Praxis®

Physical Education: Content and Design Practice Questions

Mometrix
TEST PREPARATION

Dear Future Exam Success Story

First of all, **THANK YOU** for purchasing Mometrix study materials!

Second, congratulations! You are one of the few determined test-takers who are committed to doing whatever it takes to excel on your exam. **You have come to the right place.** We developed these practice tests with one goal in mind: to deliver you the best possible approximation of the questions you will see on test day.

Standardized testing is one of the biggest obstacles on your road to success, which only increases the importance of doing well in the high-pressure, high-stakes environment of test day. Your results on this test could have a significant impact on your future, and these practice tests will give you the repetitions you need to build your familiarity and confidence with the test content and format to help you achieve your full potential on test day.

Your success is our success

We would love to hear from you! If you would like to share the story of your exam success or if you have any questions or comments in regard to our products, please contact us at **800-673-8175** or **support@mometrix.com**.

Thanks again for your business and we wish you continued success!

Sincerely,
The Mometrix Test Preparation Team

Printed in the United States of America

TABLE OF CONTENTS

PRACTICE TEST #1 ____ 1
ANSWER KEY AND EXPLANATIONS FOR TEST #1 ____ 21
PRACTICE TEST #2 ____ 40
ANSWER KEY AND EXPLANATIONS FOR TEST #2 ____ 61

Practice Test #1

1. The teacher has set up a circuit for students to engage in health-related fitness activities including muscular strength and endurance. Which of the following training measures should the teacher address to ensure safety?

a. progressive overload
b. specificity
c. regression
d. spotting

2. Jacquan would like to create a weight management program that helps him lose weight. Which of the following would help Jacquan reach his goal?

a. Energy homeostasis
b. Energy imbalance
c. Energy balance
d. Energy drinks

3. The teacher has noted that Robert is extremely competitive and regularly argues with classmates during invasion games. Which of the following strategies can minimize conflict and foster a healthy environment for all students?

a. banning Robert from invasion games
b. substituting Robert out each occurrence
c. assigning Robert to time-out
d. contracting a behavioral plan with Robert

4. Callie slips on the spilled water on the gym floor and breaks her arm during physical education class. Which of the following violations has occurred?

a. Accountability
b. Misfeasance
c. Negligence
d. Malfeasance

5. Which of the following statements best describes Bandura's social learning theory?

a. Learning through touch
b. Learning through reading
c. Learning through mental imagery
d. Learning through observation

6. Kenya is having difficulty with balance and coordination skills in the gymnastic routines. Which perceptual motor ability may be underdeveloped?

a. Hearing
b. Vision
c. Touch sensitivity
d. Audiation

7. Which of the following best describes a health effect of consuming excessive amounts of alcohol and smoking tobacco?

a. Increased risk of eating disorders
b. Increased risk of a sedentary lifestyle
c. Increased risk of heart disease
d. Increased risk of obesity

8. Which of the following best describes the relationship between ability and skill for motor performance?

a. Abilities are genetic characteristics that are the same for all.
b. Abilities are learned traits that promote skill development.
c. Abilities are genetic characteristics that impact one's ability to learn a motor skill.
d. Individuals with low ability cannot improve their motor skills.

9. Which of the following safety actions should be employed before engaging in walking, jogging, or running activities?

a. Check shoes and the surface.
b. Conduct a warm-up.
c. Check partners.
d. Put on a heart rate monitor.

10. To adapt a PE class in basketball for students with disabilities, which adaptation applies most to students using wheelchairs?

a. Play using a "beeper ball" that produces beeping sounds
b. Positioning a radio or other audio device under the basket
c. Removing any obstacles, especially small, from the court
d. Letting students hold the ball in their laps while traveling

11. Which minimum daily amounts and types of physical activity are developmentally appropriate for developing cardiovascular endurance in young children?

a. 30 minutes structured, 60 minutes unstructured daily for toddlers
b. 30 minutes structured, 60 minutes unstructured daily for preschoolers
c. 60 minutes structured, 60 minutes unstructured daily for toddlers
d. 30 minutes structured, 30 minutes unstructured daily for both age groups

12. Which of the following illustrates how recovery heart rate is used for students to assess their cardiorespiratory fitness?

a. increased heart rate recovery = less fit
b. slower heart rate recovery = more fit
c. quicker heart rate recovery = more fit
d. decreased heart rate recovery = less fit

13. Which of these is true about the National Association for Sport and Physical Education (NASPE)'s national standards for physical education?

a. They include learning and executing physical activities rather than concepts.
b. They include conducting physical activities rather than showing motor skills.
c. They include understanding concepts as well as engaging in physical activity.
d. They include valuing physical and personal but not social benefits of activity.

14. The teacher thinks a student is fabricating the need to get his inhaler during the mile run and does not allow him to get it. The student ignores the denial, retrieves the inhaler, and reports the teacher. Which of the following legal or ethical issues might the teacher encounter?

a. assumption of risk
b. breach of duty
c. proximate cause
d. damages

15. Some students with obese body mass indices are reluctant to participate during the fitness activities but are actively engaged in team sports as indicated on their heart rate monitors during game play. Which of the following can the teacher do to increase fitness participation among these students?

a. focus on health
b. focus on standards
c. focus on competitive fitness activities
d. focus on body composition

16. Which of the following safety measures are the responsibility of the teacher?

a. posting the safety rules in the gym
b. posting a link to the school-wide safety plan
c. posting the emergency exit protocols
d. posting fire drill protocols

17. The teacher probed students on how and when they get open during a game of soccer. Which of the following is the aim of the teacher's question?

a. to teach affective skills
b. to teach psychomotor skills
c. to teach tactical skills
d. to teach transfer skills

18. Michael, a 15-year-old student, has the appearance of working at a high intensity (heavy breathing, perspiring) but his heart rate monitor is consistent at 72 bpm. The teacher assigns another heart rate monitor to check for accuracy and the heart rate remains at 72 bpm. Which of the following should occur next?

a. stopping him from exercising
b. allowing him to continue exercising
c. conducting a talk test with him
d. taking his blood pressure

19. The teacher has created progressive activities where students easily find success in skill acquisition before moving on to more complex skills. Which of the following concepts is developed through this practice?

a. emotional development
b. self-regulation
c. motivation competence
d. autonomous development

20. Which of the following minimizes risks and liabilities that occur in physical education classes?

a. Routines and expectations
b. Routine professional development
c. Routine teacher observations
d. Routine inspection of equipment

21. A few students have bent legs during the cartwheel but have the flexibility to do so. Which of the following may help students improve their cartwheels?

a. observations
b. skill cues
c. yoga
d. videos

22. Which of the following curriculum approaches focuses on the fundamental movement skills needed for advanced movement skills in sport and physical activities over the lifespan?

a. Sport Education
b. Teaching Games for Understanding
c. Skill Themes
d. Cooperative Learning

23. What is a definition of body mass index (BMI)?

a. The ratio of weight to height squared
b. The ratio of abdominal fat to total fat
c. The ratio of body fat to muscle cubed
d. The ratio of total fat to overall weight

Refer to the following for questions 24–25:

For a unit on baseball, students are learning how to make a proper overhand throw. The teacher explains that the overhand throw consists of a wind up, step, rotation, and follow through. She sets up a target for students to throw their ball toward. After several rounds of unsuccessful overhand throws for some students, the teacher moves the targets closer to them. However, these students were still unable to successfully hit their target.

24. Which of the following best describes the fundamental skill category for the overhand throw?

a. Locomotor movement
b. Non-locomotor movement
c. Manipulative movement
d. Weight transfer movement

25. Which of the following is an appropriate modification for the teacher to try next?

a. Having students throw to each other
b. Keeping the targets in place until students can hit them
c. Reviewing the skill cues with the students
d. Varying the sizes of the balls thrown

26. Katherine wants to train her shoulders and neck for swim season. Which of the following exercises will meet Katherine's needs?

a. Lateral deltoid raises and shrugs
b. Shoulder curls and deltoid raises
c. Deltoid curls and shrugs
d. Anterior and rear deltoid raises

27. Which of the following best describes the appropriate duration training for a midfielder in soccer?

a. Long duration
b. Short duration
c. Intervals
d. Player specific

28. Peter and Rob are the same age, height, and weight. Peter has a high level of cardiovascular fitness, and Rob does not engage in any physical activities. Which of the following illustrates Peter's physiological responses at rest and during aerobic exercise compared to Rob?

a. Peter will have a higher heart rate and greater stroke volume during aerobic exercise.
b. Peter will have a lower heart rate and greater stroke volume during aerobic exercise.
c. Peter will have a lower heart rate and smaller stroke volume during aerobic exercise.
d. Peter will have a higher heart rate and smaller stroke volume during aerobic exercise.

29. The American Recovery and Reinvestment Act (2009) includes funding of the US Dept. of Health and Human Services to prevent chronic disease. This initiative targets which of the following as the most preventable causes of disability and death?

a. Obesity and tobacco use
b. Alcohol and tobacco use
c. Alcohol and drug use
d. Obesity and diabetes

30. Which of the following strategies will help teachers determine student progress?

a. creating an environment for self-assessment
b. conducting pre- and post-assessments
c. conducting self- and peer-assessments
d. conducting summative assessments

31. Why is it important for individuals to know the health history of their parents prior to engaging in physical activity?

a. Predisposed health conditions
b. Previous musculoskeletal injuries
c. Effects of physical activity response
d. Physical activity readiness questionnaire

32. For large classes, which of the following assessments should a teacher use to assess motor skills?

a. Checklist
b. Peer assessment
c. Self-assessment
d. Video analysis of skill proficiency

33. Researchers studying how PE teachers can influence student self-determination found all of these EXCEPT which choice?

a. Teachers' supporting student autonomy was motivating.
b. Teachers' furnishing students structure motivated them.
c. Teachers' self-determination affected their involvement.
d. Teachers' self-determination predicted that of students.

34. A first-year teacher has started at a school without a curriculum or lesson plans. Where should the teacher go for resources to help select developmentally appropriate activities for instruction?

a. Contact former physical education teachers
b. Consult state and national guidelines
c. Ask a veteran teacher
d. Ask the principal

35. What kind of validity indicates how representative a test is of every part or detail of a construct?

a. Content validity
b. Criterion validity
c. Construct validity
d. Concurrent validity

36. Which of the following is an etiquette practice expected in tennis and golf?

a. point or stroke loss for infractions
b. using the same ball throughout the game
c. silence
d. retrieving awry balls

37. Jessie rolled his ankle after landing from a basketball rebound. Which of the following first aid treatment steps should be employed?

a. elevating the injured area
b. instructing Jessie to take off his shoe
c. calling 911
d. having Jessie walk to assess the injury

38. Which of the following sport skills contain similar jumping patterns?

a. High jump and long jump
b. Volleyball spike and basketball lay-up
c. Basketball jump shot and high jump
d. Vertical jump and volleyball spike

39. What is MOST accurate about how physical education teachers can use bulletin boards to communicate instructional information to students?

a. Schools must provide real bulletin boards for physical education teachers to utilize them.
b. A time-lapse bulletin board encourages student participation and creativity.
c. A time-lapse bulletin board is a project only the physical education teacher can complete.
d. Physical education teachers must communicate orally, as students ignore bulletin boards.

40. A student recently joined a fitness center and wants to hire a personal trainer. Which of the following should the student use to evaluate the quality of the personal trainer?

a. referrals
b. body builder experience
c. a college degree
d. certification

41. A male student wants to join the dance team. His parents are extremely dissatisfied and think boys should play football. What is the best strategy the teacher can use to support the student while avoiding unnecessary conflict with the parents?

a. Respectfully tell the parents they are misinformed
b. Suggest that the student participate in both
c. Discuss the risks of playing football
d. Discuss the physical benefits of dance

42. The President's Council on Physical Fitness and Sports (2009) identifies five levels of responsibility as positive youth development goals, including the choices below. Of these, which is most related to the self-management skill of self-direction?

a. Respecting the feelings and rights of others
b. Trying out new tasks and persisting at tasks
c. Independent work, progressive goal setting
d. Democratic approaches to resolving conflict

43. What is the minimum physical activity recommended for young children?

a. A maximum of 30 minutes a day
b. A minimum of 2 hours per day
c. At most 15 minutes on most days
d. At least 60 minutes on most days

44. Which of the following strategies helps accommodate multiple abilities in physical education classes?

a. Teaching to the outcome
b. Providing extensions
c. Employing standards-based instruction
d. Incorporating differentiation

45. Which category of skills best describes kicking and dribbling?

a. Locomotor
b. Non-locomotor
c. Manipulative
d. Closed skills

46. Which of the following strategies is helpful in reducing student conflict?

a. Modeling expected behaviors
b. Using peer mediation
c. Separating the students with conflict
d. Calling the parents

47. Which of the following efforts that promote physical activity was spearheaded by a First Lady of the United States?

a. The PAN Project
b. The PACE Project
c. National PA Initiative
d. Let's Move! Initiative

48. A closeted LGBTQ student comes out in confidence to the physical education teacher. What should the teacher do with this information?

a. Contact the student's parents.
b. Contact the student's school counselor.
c. Keep quiet to maintain student trust.
d. Encourage the student to come out to peers.

49. Research finds that motor skills training, endurance training, and strength training all share which neuroplasticity effects in common?

a. New blood vessel formation
b. Motor map reorganization
c. Spinal reflex modification
d. New synapse generation

50. Which of the following is correct regarding principles of aerobic exercise?

a. Aerobic exercise involves small muscle groups.
b. Aerobic exercise entails continuous movement.
c. Aerobic exercise will firm and tone the muscles.
d. Aerobic exercise burns fat only at low intensity.

51. Compared to naturalistic observations, structured observations are ______ in physical education assessment.

a. more objective and less subjective
b. more subjective and less objective
c. more for assessing social than motor skills
d. more realistic regarding behaviors

52. Research finds cooperative learning beneficial across school subjects. It is particularly applicable to PE, which involves a high proportion of team and small-group activities. Which component of cooperative learning entails student reflection on group or team progress toward learning goals?

a. Social skills
b. Group processing
c. Individual accountability
d. Positive interdependence

53. Claire is obsessed with one of the female pop stars advertising a weight loss routine and has significantly increased her exercise. Which of the following describes Claire's behavior?

a. anorexia nervosa
b. peer pressure
c. media influence
d. community pressure

54. The English literature department has decided that Harry Potter is the book that all sixth graders will read this year. The department chair asks the PE teachers to reinforce concepts from the book in class. Which of the following approaches best describes this request?

a. Tactical approach
b. Integrated approach
c. Cooperative games approach
d. Skill themes approach

55. According to social learning theorist Albert Bandura, which of the following factors that influence observational learning most involves practicing kinesthetic and neuromuscular patterns repeatedly to imitate the teacher or other model's demonstration?

a. Attention
b. Retention
c. Reproduction
d. Reinforcement

56. In which of the following school levels is movement education most appropriate?

a. Pre-kindergarten
b. Elementary school
c. Middle school
d. High school

57. Which movement concept is the focus of locomotor and non-locomotor partner activities?

a. Relationships
b. High and low levels
c. Lead-up activities for team sports
d. Leading and following

58. Which of the following systems is responsible for excreting sweat during physical activity?

a. Immune
b. Endocrine
c. Nervous
d. Integumentary

59. Among the most prevalent challenges to kindergarten through Grade 12 physical education, which has recently become even more challenging than the others?

a. Inadequate resources and parental support
b. Overly large class sizes and teacher burnout
c. Violence, student drug abuse, and discipline
d. Reductions in school curriculum times for physical education

60. Which of the following is least likely to cause a sudden academic decline:

a. Parental divorce
b. Drug abuse
c. Eating disorders
d. Participation in a school sports team

61. A student sprains an ankle after landing from a balance beam jump. Which of the following is the first priority immediately after a student sprains an ankle?

a. Mobilizing the injury
b. Putting ice on the injury
c. Putting heat on the injury
d. Calling 911

62. Among movement skill competencies reflecting developmental standards, which is most suitable for students in the fifth grade?

a. Moving creatively to varied musical rhythms using simple dance steps
b. Jumping rope to the tempo of music, both singly and with a partner
c. Bouncing, passing, and catching a ball, matching a musical rhythm
d. Expressing feelings, ideas in rhythmic motion with, without music

63. Which of the following steps used in jazz dance is similar to the gallop?

a. chasse
b. axel
c. ball change
d. the drop

64. The teacher has planned a hiking unit to take advantage of the neighboring hiking trails. Which of the following is a procedural issue that should be employed?

a. Applying sunscreen
b. Assigning a student-leader
c. Charging the teacher's cell phone
d. Taking attendance

65. Which of the following strategies fosters teamwork?

a. Having team captains
b. Goal setting
c. Meeting with players individually
d. Watching videos of gameplay

66. During practice, John made all of his free throws. During the game, John missed all of his free throws. Which type of constraints likely impacted John's performance negatively?

a. Individual and functional constraints
b. Individual and environmental constraints
c. Individual and task constraints
d. Individual and biological constraints

67. Which of the following best describes the motor skills used in basketball, tennis, and floor hockey?

a. Manipulative skills
b. Offensive skills
c. Closed skills
d. Defensive skills

68. The federal government defines basic elements of furthering student development through physical activity (PA) that PE programs and teachers promote. How are these elements structured to accomplish major PE goals?

a. Attaining participant developmental health outcomes enables creating optimum contexts for PA, which enables providing universal PA opportunities and access.
b. Creating optimum contexts for PA enables providing universal PA opportunities and access, which enables attaining participant developmental health outcomes.
c. Providing universal PA opportunities and access enables creating optimum contexts for PA, which enables attaining participant developmental health outcomes.
d. Attaining participant developmental health outcomes enables providing universal PA opportunities and access, which enables creating optimum contexts for PA.

69. Which of the following is an appropriate method used to assess heart rate (HR) intensity during exercise?

a. Continuous aerobic activity
b. Talk test
c. Percentage of maximum heart rate
d. Recovery heart rate

70. Out of 30 students, 10 are advanced, 10 are intermediate, and 10 are beginners. Which of the following strategies best accommodates mixed-ability students for skill development and refinement?

a. Skill choice
b. Varied skill circuits
c. Combined skill grouping
d. Partner advanced and beginner students

71. Which of the following is an example of a psychological approach that aims to develop intrinsic student motivation in physical education?

a. Self-determination theory
b. Behaviorism theory
c. Social theory
d. Constructivism theory

72. Which of the following is the purpose of assessment in physical education programs?

a. To assess teacher effectiveness
b. To assess lesson plans
c. To measure learning
d. To measure objectives

73. Compared to the amount of time in moderate to vigorous physical activity (MVPA) the Institute of Medicine recommends for children to spend daily, how much do research studies find they actually spend in school physical education classes?

a. About one-sixth of what is recommended
b. About one-third of what is recommended
c. About one-half of what is recommended
d. About the same as is recommended

74. When learning new PE skills, students need more _____ feedback; when they have developed more competence and confidence in certain PE skills and can analyze their own performance, they can make better use of _____ feedback.

a. Extrinsic; intrinsic
b. Intrinsic; extrinsic
c. Positive; negative
d. Constructive; corrective

75. Among the following statements, which is accurate regarding several illnesses of early childhood?

a. The human parvovirus infection causing fifth disease is serious, and children always show symptoms.
b. Respiratory syncytial virus (RSV) is both more common and more problematic to children than the flu.
c. Human hand, foot, and mouth disease is rare in childhood, is caused by bacteria, and is quite serious.
d. About 6% of young children get croup annually, up to 25% are hospitalized, and it is frequently lethal.

76. Students are having difficulty striking the tennis ball with the tennis racket. Which of the following will help students improve their performance?

a. Striking the ball while it is airborne
b. Using a larger ball
c. Moving closer to the net
d. Earlier preparation

77. A bowler is capable of hitting the middle pin relatively consistently. What is one way they can improve their success at making strikes?

a. Using a heavier ball
b. Moving further to the left
c. Putting more spin on the ball
d. Throwing the ball from farther away

78. Jumping fast and landing softly best describe which movement concepts?

a. Strong and weak
b. Strong and forceful
c. Tempo and force
d. Time and speed

79. Which of the following stretching practices has shown to have the greatest improvements in flexibility?

a. active stretching
b. PNF stretching
c. ballistic stretching
d. dynamic stretching

80. Which of the following is a health risk when endurance training in the heat?

a. Increase in heart rate
b. Increase in sweat production
c. Hyperthermia
d. Hypothermia

81. According to experts, what is true about the primary functions of nonverbal communication?

a. Nonverbal communication serves a function of performing social rituals.
b. Nonverbal communication shows personalities rather than relationships.
c. Nonverbal communication is used to replace, not help, verbal interaction.
d. Nonverbal communication is not used like words for expressing feelings.

82. Some female students avoid weight training exercises for fear of getting very large and looking more masculine. Which of the following is an appropriate response to these students to dispel this myth?

a. inform them to use bodyweight in lieu of free weights
b. inform them that it is possible to get stronger without getting bulky
c. inform them that their nutrition intake would need to greatly increase
d. partner them with female students who weight train but are not abnormally large

Refer to the following for question 83:

A student playing as a goalie in soccer is having difficulty punting the ball. He takes two steps, drops the ball from waist height, leans back, and kicks the bottom of the ball with the toe of his shoe. During one of his attempts, he accidentally punts the ball at his teammate Tracy, causing her nose to begin bleeding.

83. Which of the following protocols should be immediately employed before sending Tracy to the nurse?

a. Instruct her to blow their nose
b. Instruct her to get a pair of gloves
c. Instruct her to pinch their nose
d. Instruct her to hold their head back

84. To improve cardiovascular health, what is the recommended amount of cardiovascular activity for children and adults?

a. 20 minutes for adults and 45 minutes for children, three days a week
b. 20 minutes for adults and 30 minutes for children, most days of the week
c. 10 minutes for adults and 20 minutes for children, three days a week
d. 30 minutes for adults and 60 minutes for children, most days of the week

85. Of the following beliefs common among high school students about exercise, nutrition, and health, which is accurate rather than a misconception or myth?

a. Eat simple carbs after exercising.
b. Everybody should take vitamins.
c. Drink eight glasses of water per day.
d. Vitamins supply greater energy.

86. Among elements of the FITT principle, which one is determined by two of the others?

a. How long each workout session should last
b. How to ensure overload without overwork
c. How often to work out for stress plus rest
d. How training is cardio, resistance, or both

87. Which type of practice is most effective for preparing athletes for the unpredictable situations encountered in team sports?

a. Variable practice
b. Massed practice
c. Distributed practice
d. Blocked practice

88. Research-based strategies to motivate students are reflected by which teacher behavior?

a. They are interested in students' learning but are not personally interested.
b. They are role models, leading student motivation and passion by example.
c. They need not believe in students' abilities as long as they indicate interest.
d. They eschew the personalization of subject content for individual students.

89. Among progressive-resistance exercises, which of the following uses the largest number and variety of equipment?

a. Free weight work
b. Partner resistance
c. Body weight training
d. Circuit weight training

90. A student recovering from a knee injury has medical clearance to engage in physical education. Which of the following modifications are recommended for cardiovascular activities?

a. Excuse the student from exercises that involve jumps.
b. Allow the student to choose from a list of exercises.
c. Refrain from activities until the knee has completely healed.
d. Allow the student to assess peers in cardiovascular activities.

91. Which activity best promotes strength in the quadriceps muscles?

a. Abductors with added weight
b. Bridges with added weight
c. Deadlifts with added weight
d. Squats with added weight

92. Which of the following exercises best trains the shoulders?

a. Lat pulls
b. Lateral deltoid raises
c. Overhead triceps extensions
d. Shrugs

93. The target heart rate zone, which is attained through moderate-intensity activity, improves aerobic capacity, energy, and fitness, and burns fat, is which percentage of an individual's maximum heart rate?

a. 50-65 percent
b. 85-100 percent
c. 50 percent or less
d. 65-85 percent

94. Students track and reflect on their successes, failures, and engagement with classmates during the ball handling activities, and rate their performance at the end of class. Which of the following teaching models is evident in these tasks?

a. Cooperative learning
b. Guided discovery
c. SEL
d. TPSR

95. After tracking his teaching behaviors, Mr. Green realized that taking attendance for 40 students takes up a lot of time, which reduces student engagement. How might Mr. Green alter his attendance taking method to increase the opportunities for students to respond?

a. set a time-limit to take attendance
b. practice taking attendance faster
c. take attendance during the warm-up
d. take attendance in squad lines

96. For a student who has joint problems but wants to be physically active, which is the best extracurricular activity?

a. Skiing
b. Swimming
c. Skateboarding
d. Playing soccer

97. The teacher consistently provides direct verbal and demonstrative feedback to beginning students. What is the purpose of using these feedback strategies?

a. To diversify feedback delivery
b. To help students practice the desired outcome
c. To help students perfect the desired outcome
d. To help students understand the desired outcome

98. Which of the following physiological adaptations do cardiovascular activities induce?

a. less reliance on glucose
b. heart size increases
c. decrease in blood volume
d. lactic acid build-up

99. Which of the following best describes the cooperative learning approach?

a. Competitive collaboration
b. Non-competitive collaboration
c. Peer activities
d. Group activities

100. When is performing the Heimlich maneuver on a student indicated?

a. The student says he or she is having trouble breathing.
b. The student is choking and is not able to breathe.
c. The student has trouble breathing and is coughing.
d. The student is not responding to cardiopulmonary resuscitation (CPR).

101. Withdrawal, declining grades, sudden changes in behavior, and poor hygiene are all potential indicators of what?

a. Peer pressure in the classroom
b. A developmental delay or learning disability
c. A social or emotional disorder
d. Abuse or neglect in the home

102. Which of the following fitness tracking devices can inform the teacher of the intensity of students' movements?

a. Heart rate monitor
b. Accelerometer
c. Pedometer
d. Step counter

103. Which of the following fitness activities are students engaged in when participating in orienteering?

a. Walking, hiking, and swimming
b. Walking, cycling, and swimming
c. Walking, jogging, and running
d. Swimming, cycling, and running

104. The cross-country coach had a spaghetti dinner for the team the night before a competition. Which of the following is the rationale for this activity?

a. To recruit energy fast
b. To run on an empty stomach
c. To ensure an equitable, healthy meal
d. To aid in better sleep

105. Which of the following is a defensive running pattern common in dual and team sports?

a. high level
b. zigzags
c. transitions
d. curves

106. As students enter adolescence, their social lives will most likely take on which of the following characteristics?

a. Desire to spend most of their time with immediate family members
b. Membership in a small social group that has a shared set of values and interests
c. Marked rise in insecurity resulting from increased threats of violence
d. Decreased interest in ethnic and cultural identity

107. Blake complains of delayed onset muscle soreness after working out for the first time in three months. Which principle of fitness best describes Blake's condition?

a. Progression
b. Overload
c. Reversibility
d. Regression

108. Basic principles of physical fitness include Overload and FITT. When combining these two, which of the following can be changed for BOTH resistance (weight) training AND cardiovascular (aerobic) training?

a. Changing the workout by doing different exercises
b. Increasing the number of repetitions to complete
c. Increasing the resistance or weight being pressed
d. Increasing the number of days when working out

109. Cardiovascular endurance training in hot environments can cause heat illnesses. Which of these is the most severe kind?

a. Heat exhaustion
b. Heat cramps
c. Dehydration
d. Heat stroke

110. Ms. Paul notices that many girls never have the ball in possession long enough to develop ball-handling skills during team sports games. What strategy can provide girls with opportunities to develop ball-handling skills?

a. Stop teaching team sports activities.
b. Add a rule that girls must touch the ball at least once before scoring.
c. Practice ball-handling skills in isolation.
d. Allow girls to play amongst themselves.

111. Katherine felt her body over rotate during the shotput. Which of the following types of feedback describes Katherine's experience?

a. knowledge of performance
b. knowledge of results
c. positive transfer
d. negative transfer

112. Which of the following safety practices is recommended in dance?

a. dynamic warm-up
b. static movements
c. loose clothing
d. yoga stretches

113. Which of the following systems is responsible for producing the white blood cells in the body?

a. The integumentary system
b. The nervous system
c. The circulatory system
d. The lymphatic system

114. Bobby is unhappy that he lost his starting position and is lashing out at his replacement. What is the primary reason the coach should work on teamwork strategies?

a. Teamwork aids in achieving team goals
b. Teamwork is required for success in life
c. Teamwork teaches responsibility
d. Teamwork teaches players about their role

115. Of the following, which elementary school activity best integrates physical education skills with English language arts (ELA) skills within the same lesson?

a. Students perform movements and then look up adverbs and write synonyms and antonyms.
b. Students look up and write adverbs, synonyms, and antonyms and then perform movements.
c. Students identify adverbs in teacher-read sentences and describe movements using adverbs.
d. Students perform movements in ways described by recently learned adverbs on given cards.

116. Which of the following safety considerations should be employed during a jumping and landing unit?

a. Feet shoulder-distance apart on the landing
b. Feet side by side on the landing
c. Soft or bent knees on the landing
d. Locked knees for a secure landing

117. In creating a positive climate for PE student learning activities, which of the following accurately reflects an expert recommendation or principle?

a. Increasing learning opportunities creates a positive climate.
b. Teachers must use a few motivational strategies uniformly.
c. Students must already have learned appropriate behaviors.
d. Holding students accountable destroys the positive climate.

118. Which type of muscle is responsible for voluntary muscular contraction that occurs during physical activity?

a. Smooth
b. Skeletal
c. Cardiac
d. Sliding filament

119. Stephanie started a workout routine for her New Year's resolution. Her body was extremely sore and she could barely walk the next day. Which of the following principles of fitness did Stephanie ignore?

a. Delayed onset muscle syndrome
b. Overload
c. Progression
d. Specificity

120. Which of the following techniques to measure aerobic duration is appropriate for large class sizes?

a. Activity trackers
b. Pedometers
c. Stopwatches
d. Aerobic equipment monitors

121. Physical education is under attack by a powerful parent group who believe physical education is only fun and games. Which of the following laws can be used to explain to parents the impact of physical education?

a. Title IX
b. IDEA
c. SHAPE America toolkit
d. ESSA

122. Which statement best reflects factors that can interfere with diverse parents' and families' communication and participation in their children's education??

a. Language barriers rarely stop parents/families from communicating.
b. Parents with unsuccessful school histories try harder to participate.
c. Families can be alienated from school processes because of culture.
d. Poor past school experiences induce parents to help their children.

123. Which of the following is a benefit of progressive partner-resistance exercises?

a. The muscle being trained is less isolated.
b. They are safer on the muscle trained.
c. They have a considerably lower risk of injury than normal resistance training.
d. Equipment is not required for the muscle trained.

124. When teaching a novice batter, the teacher should focus on which of the following?

a. Demonstrations and verbal instructions on the skills task
b. Vary distances to strike the ball
c. Opportunities for the batter to pitch the ball
d. Game-like scenarios for students to practice batting

125. Which statement is most accurate about the roles of teacher praise and criticism relative to student motivation and encouragement?

a. Teachers praising student efforts frequently encourage students.
b. Teachers judiciously choosing what to praise encourage students.
c. Teachers praising students too freely inhibit their self-motivation.
d. Teachers who give students any kind of criticism discourage them.

126. Which of the following is a strategy used for refinement and integration of manipulative skills?

a. mirroring
b. choice
c. leading and following
d. small-sided games

127. Which of the following best describes the purpose of the Presidential Youth Fitness and FitnessGram® programs?

a. To assess health-related fitness
b. To assess skill-related fitness
c. To assess health- and skill-related fitness
d. To assess dynamic fitness and sports skills

128. Several students walk with rounded shoulders or hunched backs. Which of the following exercises will foster good posture and flexibility?

a. curl-ups
b. back extensions
c. pectorals deck
d. lateral raises

129. During individual sports, the player does not have teammates to rely on. Which of the following attributes is generally the most important for success in individual sports?

a. Positive transfer from team sports
b. Leadership
c. Communication
d. Self-efficacy

130. What advantages does Fitbit technology include for physical education teachers and students?

a. Weight control but not sleep quality
b. Self-monitoring but not competition
c. Fashion appeal as well as motivation
d. Charts and graphs available offline

Answer Key and Explanations for Test #1

1. A: The teacher should address the concept of progressive overload, which is the gradual increase in weight. Students should start with low weight and gradually increase to prevent injury and extreme soreness. In circuit training, various exercises are specific to the muscle group or health-related fitness component but are general for group circuits. Specificity is not a safety measure. Regression is the principle of "if you don't use it, you lose it," or you regress or lose the gains made from training if you stop engaging in fitness activities. Spotting is a safety measure but not done during circuit training typically as the pace of activities is too fast and designed to get through several exercises quickly. Spotting is ideal for muscular strength activities that require lifting heavy amounts like squats or bench presses performed at a slower pace.

2. B: Jacquan needs to create an energy imbalance where he burns more fuel or calories than food or calorie consumption. Energy balance (C), or homeostasis (A), is equal amounts of energy in and energy out and is ideal for individuals who want to maintain their current weight. Energy drinks (D) often contain excessive amounts of sugar and caffeine. They are not generally recommended to include in a weight loss program, as too much sugar can impede weight-loss goals.

3. C: Assigning Robert to take a time-out will minimize conflict and foster a healthy environment for all students. Substituting Robert out may send a mixed-message and Robert may not associate the substitution as a result of his behavior as subbing is part of invasion gameplay. To ban Robert from invasion games is an approach that restricts Robert from getting an education; however, a temporary ban may be appropriate for chronic or a certain number of offenses. Calling Robert's parents and developing a contract or behavioral plan with Robert is a strategy used after in-class classroom strategies are unsuccessful. A behavioral plan is co-created with the student or students that includes expectations and consequences for infractions.

4. C: Negligence has occurred as the teacher did not ensure a safe environment by cleaning the spill. While not intentional, the teacher may be held liable. Accountability (A) is holding the teacher to certain standards. There may be a consequence for the incident. The circumstance may also be considered an accident where the teacher can be given a reminder to check the floors throughout instruction, especially after water breaks. Misfeasance (B) is a type of negligence that occurs when a teacher incorrectly implements a policy or practice. Malfeasance (D) is an act where the teacher intentionally breaks the law.

5. D: Bandura's social learning theory is also known as observational learning theory, where watching someone's performance through modeling and demonstration as well as receiving feedback impact learning. Learning through touch, reading, and mental imagery also aid in learning but are not a part of observational learning theory.

6. B: Vision is the perceptual motor ability that aids in movement detection and movement response. If Kenya is closing her eyes, that may be causing increased balance and coordination difficulty, as those sensory responses are not activated. Hearing perception is important for motor skill development but is more closely related to the body preparing to take action, for example, when hearing "go" or "start," or the sound of a thrown or caught ball.

7. C: Excessive alcohol consumption and smoking tobacco both increase the risk of heart disease. Living a sedentary or inactive lifestyle also increases the risk of heart disease and has been associated with similar poor health outcomes as smoking. Alcohol consists of empty calories and can contribute to the risk of excessive weight gain, leading to obesity. Eating disorders like anorexia nervosa or bulimia are psychological conditions with significant body image dissatisfaction and irrational fears of becoming overweight or obese.

8. C: Abilities predominantly result from the genetic make-up of an individual, which varies among students in physical education. With practice, most individuals can improve their motor skills, but the degree of improvement is contingent upon their abilities.

9. A: Before engaging in walking, jogging, and running activities, shoes should be checked for wear and shoelaces should be tied. The surface should be inspected for dust, dirt, cracks, trash, objects (e.g., glass), uneven surfaces, and other potential hazards. A warm-up is not always necessary for walking or jogging; they are already considered warm-up activities due to their light to moderate intensity. However, one or both can serve as a warm-up activity for running.

10. D: Students using wheelchairs need their hands to propel them (or press buttons or switches controlling power chairs) and cannot dribble a ball simultaneously, so letting them hold the ball in their laps while traveling is an adaptation. Using a "beeper ball" (a), putting a radio under the basket (b), and removing small obstacles from the court (c) are all basketball adaptations for students with visual impairments.

11. A: Experts recommend that toddlers have at least 30 minutes of structured physical activity (PA) and at least 60 minutes of unstructured PA daily. For preschoolers, the recommendation is 60 minutes of structured PA and at least 60 minutes of unstructured PA daily, not 30/60 (B); hence 60/60 is NOT advised for toddlers (C). The recommendations are NOT the same for both age groups (D), and 30 minutes of unstructured PA is insufficient for either.

12. C: A fast heart rate recovery suggests that a person is more fit than someone with slow heart rate recovery. Heart rate recovery is how fast the heart rate decreases after cardiovascular exercise, taken in 1-minute, 2-minute, or 3-minute intervals. For example, a recovery heart rate of 60 beats in one minute (an excellent rate of recovery) is better than a recovery rate at 30 beats in one minute (a good rate of recovery). Therefore, the higher the recovery heart rate after exercise indicates good cardiorespiratory fitness or a healthy heart. A slow heart rate recovery (less than 25 bpm) increases death risk and is attributed to poor cardiovascular health. With consistent cardiovascular training, heart rate recovery will become faster.

13. C: The NASPE's national standards for physical education include both understanding the main concepts, principles, methods, and techniques of movement and also engaging regularly in physical activity; hence, they do not exclude concepts (A). In addition to engaging in physical activity, these standards also include that an individual be able to demonstrate the motor skills (B) required for doing so. As well as valuing the physical and personal benefits of exercising, these standards include seeing value in the social benefits of physical activity (D), such as the opportunities that it offers for engaging in social interactions.

14. B: The teacher breached duty or teacher responsibilities that includes maintaining a safe environment for all students. The teacher put this student's health and potentially life at risk. Assumption of risk is a defense against negligence and is when the student or participant agrees to engage in an activity that has an element of risk, such as in the extreme example of sky diving. Since students do not choose the activities done in most physical education classes, the assumption of risk defense is unlikely to be used in physical education cases. Proximate cause is another defense against negligence and suggests that accidents and injury would transpire with or without the teacher's presence. For damages to be awarded to the student or his family, he would have had to sustain injury, fatality, or suffer emotional harm.

15. C: For these students, achieving fitness through team sports is a more realistic goal. The teacher can employ competitive or team fitness activities where the focus is on a team goal rather than health, the standards, or body composition. Obese students tend to dislike physical education and physical activities due to bodies on display and the promotion of thinness or normal weight body mass indices, which are more pronounced during fitness activities. The teacher can provide instruction that promotes health and use the standards in a team-based approach, but doing so during traditional fitness activities may ostracize student engagement, especially when focusing on body composition.

16. A: The teacher is responsible for informing students of the safety rules and posting the rules around the gym. The teacher can provide links to school-wide information as a courtesy, but the school leadership team is responsible for disseminating safety plans to parents and students. School leadership personnel are also required to have emergency exit and fire drill protocols posted. The teacher is responsible for implementing fire drill expectations.

17. C: The teacher aims to develop tactical skills or decision-making and action skills required for effective gameplay. Psychomotor skills are actions or movements only. Transfer skills occur in invasion games but the question is specific to soccer and not invasion games generally. Affective skills would include attitudes, feelings, and values for soccer.

18. A: Michael should stop working out and go to the nurse to make sure there is no medical issue. Allowing him to continue exercising may pose harm. A talk test is another tool used to determine intensity, but the heart rate monitor is more accurate and supersedes the talk test. While blood pressure and heart rate are health indicators, they do not increase at the same rates. A low heart rate is not an indicator of hypertension; therefore, taking his blood pressure would be meaningless.

19. C: Motivation competence is developed when students experience success in easier tasks that builds confidence to try more difficult tasks. Self-regulation is awareness of how one learns and acceptance of the responsibility for the learning. Emotional development is the ability to manage feelings and emotions to focus on learning. Autonomous development is when learners perform tasks easily or automatically, as they have mastered the skill and no longer have to think about it.

20. D: Routine inspection of equipment helps minimize risks and liabilities that occur in physical education. Routines and expectations are classroom management and instructional strategies. Rules and safety practices would aid in minimizing risks and liabilities common in physical education classes. Routine professional development is offered to help teachers improve student learning. Routine teacher observations are conducted to provide feedback to the teacher on success, progress, and any areas for improvement.

21. D: Students are likely to improve if they "see" themselves perform the cartwheel with bent legs to help them focus when they perform the cartwheel, again. Observations and skill cues are usually the first stages of instruction, so it is evident that these options have not helped. Since students are already flexible, yoga would not be an activity that would help them improve.

22. C: The Skill Themes approach focuses on teaching the fundamental movement skills (e.g., catching and throwing; running and sliding) required to perform more complex movements needed for sport and leisure activities. Sport Education is an approach to teaching team sports where every student has a role, such as player, coach, referee, or scorekeeper, which changes when starting a new "season" or the next sport. Teaching Games for Understanding (TGfU) is a tactical approach to teaching team sports that involves creating an environment where students have to make decisions during gameplay. Cooperative learning is a student-centered approach where students work together towards a common goal. Cooperative learning activities are evident or can be implemented in many curriculum approaches including the ones aforementioned.

23. A: Body mass index (BMI) is the ratio of weight to height squared, which shows the relationship between a person's weight and height. It is not the ratio of abdominal to total fat (B), fat to muscle (C), or fat to weight (D). Healthy BMIs are generally between 18.5 and 24.9. Below 18.5 is considered underweight, and 25 to 29.9 is considered overweight (with a few exceptions; e.g., some people with very high muscle mass rather than fat may have higher BMIs). A BMI of 30 or above is considered obese.

24. C: The overhand throw is a manipulative movement skill that combines non-locomotor or locomotor movement with an object or equipment. Locomotor movements are traveling movements that get a person from point A to point B. Non-locomotor movements are movements without traveling. While weight transfer is done during the overhand throw, weight transfer is a movement concept and not a fundamental skill category.

25. D: The teacher should vary the sizes of the balls thrown as students may not be able to grip the balls used. Having students throw to each other is no different than throwing at a target, and if positioned at the same distance, the ball will still not reach. Keeping the targets in place does not solve the problem. Reviewing skill cues is appropriate, but skill cues are not modifications of the task.

26. A: Katherine should incorporate lateral deltoid raises to target the shoulders and shrugs to target the trapezius (the muscle group connecting the neck and shoulders) to prepare for the swim season. Deltoid raises can be performed laterally, posteriorly, and anteriorly, but lateral deltoid raises also work the trapezius muscles. Shoulder joint actions include flexion, extension, adduction, and abduction, but the shoulder joint is not capable of a curling action.

27. C: The appropriate training schedule for a midfielder in soccer is interval training with the Fartlek method of switching between random speeds consisting of short sprints, running downfield, walking, and jogging. These are helpful because movements in soccer can vary drastically. Long duration training is more appropriate for endurance activities including cross country and cycling. Short duration training is more appropriate for short or explosive activities, e.g., the 100-meter sprint and jumping. Duration training is specific to the game or position rather than the player.

28. B: Regular engagement in aerobic activities aids in cardiovascular fitness. Physiological adaptations that occur include a lower heart rate both at rest and during exercise and a greater stroke volume. The heart becomes stronger as a result of cardiovascular fitness and is able to force or pump blood (stroke volume) throughout the body with less effort.

29. A: The US Dept. of HHS targets obesity and tobacco use as the most preventable causes of disability and death. Alcohol use (B and C) also causes disability and death but is not one of HHS' targets in the prevention initiative. Drug abuse (C) is also not a target of this initiative. Diabetes (D) causes disability and death; however, type 1 diabetes is genetic or organic, while type 2 diabetes is largely caused by obesity, which is a target.

30. B: To determine student progress, the teacher should conduct a pre- and post-assessment, which will aid in determining if progress has been made or whether the teacher needs to alter instruction or reevaluate the assessments. Self- and peer-assessments are ongoing formative assessments done between the pre- and post-assessments to help students understand content and movement patterns. A summative assessment is the final or post-assessment done at the end of the unit, which assesses a student's knowledge, but when conducted independently of a pre-assessment, progress cannot be established definitively.

31. A: Some medical conditions, such as hypertension, can be exacerbated by engaging in certain physical activities; therefore, it is important to know if participants are predisposed to or have hereditary health conditions to ensure a safe exercise environment. Musculoskeletal injuries are generally the result of overtraining, muscle overuse, awkward movements, colliding with a person or object, or are age-related, such as with osteoporosis.

32. A: For large classes, a checklist of skills is the fastest method to assess motor skills. This checklist can be in the format of a rubric, with particular performance activities or behaviors to look for, making the assessment efficient to quantify and look for in large groups of students. Peer and self-assessments are excellent strategies to help students gain understanding of skill performance but should not be used for the instructor's evaluation of skills because they can be objective or unreliable. Video analysis of skills is an effective strategy to assess skills, but this method is slow and time-consuming and not ideal to assess skills when there is a faster method to choose from for large class sizes.

33. D: Researchers have found that when teachers used motivational strategies of supporting student autonomy (a), providing structure (b), and being involved (i.e., demonstrating interest and emotional support), their strategy use was predicted by teacher perceptions of student self-determination; teacher self-determination affected this prediction (c); and student perceptions of teacher motivational strategies and student satisfaction with their own competence and autonomy improved student self-determination. However, they found that teacher self-determination did NOT predict student self-determination (d).

34. B: The first-year teacher should consult the state- and national-level physical education guidelines. Each state has a physical education association with physical education guidelines, and SHAPE America provides national physical education guidelines, standards, and recommendations. Unless the principal was a physical education teacher, they are not a content expert. Former or veteran physical education teachers may not be abreast of current guidelines, standards, and best practices.

35. A: Content validity is how representative a test is of every single component of the construct it measures. Criterion validity is how well a test measures an outcome in comparison to a standard. Construct validity is how representative a test is of a certain construct it is designed to measure (e.g., if it is meant to measure depression, it should not measure anxiety). Concurrent validity is a subtype of criterion validity in which the measure in question and the established standard are carried out at the same time.

36. D: An etiquette practice in golf and tennis is to retrieve any ball that goes awry. Silence is an expected etiquette practice during a serve in tennis and during the stroke in golf, but once the ball is struck, lands, or after a point is earned, it is acceptable for the crowd and spectators to cheer. It is a rule, not a matter of etiquette, for players to use the same ball in golf and balls in tennis unless the balls get lost or damaged. Another rule or penalty in tennis and golf is to lose a point or stroke for infractions.

37. A: Jessie should elevate the injured area to reduce swelling and inflammation. It would be better for Jessie to keep his shoe on for support, compression, and inflammation reduction. Removing his shoe may increase the risk of swelling and further injury. A call to 911 would occur for a severe or life-threatening injury. Jessie should sit down or rest the injured area, as walking can cause further damage.

38. D: The vertical jump and volleyball spike have a similar jumping pattern because they are accomplished by jumping upward with two feet. The high jump uses a one-foot take off in a curved position; the long jump also uses a one-foot take-off, but the body propels horizontally with the feet leading. A basketball lay-up uses a one-foot take-off, and a volleyball spike and jump shot use a two-foot take-off.

39. B: A time-lapse bulletin board can begin with the physical education (PE) teacher labeling a board's theme (e.g., balance, strength, speed, teamwork, sportsmanship, a certain sport, etc.) posting about a dozen pictures to provide examples and ideas for students and get them started. The teacher then assigns students to bring in pictures—drawings, photos, diagrams, art, and so on that they have found or made—that apply to the board's identified theme. Over time, student contributions fill the board with pictures, which students can view, discuss, and use as illustrations to help them understand aspects of a learning unit or topic. PE teachers need not even have schools provide (A) or have to buy their own real bulletin boards; they simply can create a board by hanging large pieces of paper, poster board, or fabric on the wall. This project is completed by students, not just teachers (C). Students do not ignore such boards (D), especially when they contain their own and classmates' contributions.

40. D: When hiring a personal trainer, the student should check to see if the personal trainer is certified, the certification agency, and if the certification is current as personal training certifications require cognitive knowledge and practical application of skills. A college degree is not required to become a certified personal trainer and does not guarantee that the trainer has knowledge of personal training concepts and skills. However, a college degree in a physical activity field, e.g., physical education, kinesiology, or exercise and sport science, is required for the more reputable personal training certification agencies. Experience in body building or fitness training and referrals help with advertising and marketing but do not indicate the level of knowledge that the trainer has.

41. D: Informing parents of the physical benefits of dance, careers in dance, and perhaps male role models in dance may help change their perceptions (stereotypes) that boys/males do not or should not engage in dance. Discussing the risks of playing football could be a strategy, but the parents may find this offensive because they are pro-football and may see the benefits as outweighing the risks. Suggesting that the student participate in both does not necessarily support the student because he may not want to play football. Telling parents that they are wrong will likely be offensive and negatively impact the teacher-parent relationship.

42. C: Levels of responsibility defining positive youth development goals incorporate self-management skills, including **self-control**, exemplified by respecting others' feeling and rights (a) and approaching conflict resolution democratically (d); **self-motivation**, shown in trying out new tasks and persistence on tasks (b) and exemplifying effort; and **self-direction**, exemplified by working independently, setting goals progressively (c), and resisting peer pressure.

43. D: Experts recommend that young children have at least 60 minutes of physical activity on most days. This is important for strengthening bones, muscles including the heart, and lungs; developing gross motor skills; ensuring better sleep; developing social skills; reinforcing family bonds through family playtimes; having fun and improving children's moods; and boosting children's self-images and self-esteem through pride at physical attainments. Minimums of 30 (A) or 15 (C) minutes are not enough physical activity for young children. Two hours (B) of physical activity is not the recommended minimum.

44. D: Differentiation is a strategy that addresses multiple abilities that exist in one class. The teacher should have activities for beginner, intermediate, and advanced students to meet all learners' needs and include extensions and remediations. Some students have mastered or exceeded the learning outcome but still need to be challenged and learn new ways of doing things.

45. C: Manipulative skills are a combination of locomotor (traveling) and non-locomotor (bending) movements while using equipment (ball, hockey stick or puck, balance beam). Manipulative skills involve both gross motor and fine motor movements. For instance, when kicking and dribbling in soccer, tapping with the feet engages the fine motor muscles. During the kick, often conducted while walking or running (locomotor), the knee and waist bend (non-locomotor).

46. A: Modeling expected behaviors is a strategy that reduces student conflict. Students often engage in behaviors they see rather than the ones they told are correct. Peer mediation is a strategy used to solve student conflict after it has already occurred. Separating students might be a temporary measure used as a cooling-off period but is also implemented after the conflict. Furthermore, cooperation and working with others are fundamental objectives in most physical education programs, and separating students is not an appropriate long-term solution. Calling the parents is an informative response to conflict that has already transpired but is unnecessary to conduct before any potential conflict.

47. D: First Lady Michelle Obama started the Let's Move! Initiative (2010), promoting physical activity (PA) to combat the obesity epidemic and improve child and teen health. The International Life Sciences Institute (ILSI) Research Foundation started the Physical Activity and Nutrition (PAN) Project for Adolescents (a). The Physician Assessment and Counseling for Exercise (PACE) Project (b) developed tools for primary-care physicians to counsel PA for patients, and researches and develops tools for individuals, healthcare systems, and providers. The US Centers for Disease Control and Prevention (CDC) started the National PA Initiative (c) to reduce chronic disease risk factors.

48. C: The teacher should keep quiet to maintain the student's trust. It is also not the teacher's responsibility to tell students' sexualities, regardless of where they land on the sexuality continuum. Contacting the student's parents could put the student in harm's way if the parents are not accepting. Unless there is evidence of the student harming themselves, there is no need to contact the school counselor. Contacting the counselor for LGBTQ resources is appropriate; however, the student's identity should remain confidential. Only the student should be allowed to decide if or when to come out. Therefore, the teacher should refrain from encouraging the student to do so.

49. C: Research studies find that motor skills, endurance, and strength training all modify the spinal reflexes according to the specific behaviors each task requires. New blood vessels are formed (A) through endurance training but not motor skills or strength training. Motor maps are reorganized (B) through motor skills training but not endurance or strength training. New synapses are primarily generated (D) through motor skills training but not endurance training.

50. B: For exercise to be aerobic, it must involve continuous movement, not stop-and-start movement, to elevate the heart and respiratory rates for sustained durations. Aerobic exercise uses the large muscle groups, not small (a). It typically does NOT firm or tone muscles (c) due to low resistance; weight training does. Another common misconception is that aerobic exercise must be of low intensity to burn fat (d); research finds sufficient exercise at any intensity can reduce fat.

51. A: Structured observations involve informing both teacher and student of the observation and applying specific criteria for evaluating student performance in physical education (PE) assessment. Naturalistic observations involve not informing students of the observation to capture typical student behavior, such as during their daily practice in regular PE classes. Though naturalistic observations are more realistic regarding behaviors than structured observations, not vice versa (D), they have been criticized for being more subjective, whereas structured observations are more objective, not vice versa (B). Structured observations are equally good for assessing social skills, motor skills (C), and movement skills.

52. B: Among cooperative learning components, social skills (a) are incorporated such that students can identify their purposes and applications. Group processing (b) entails student reflection on how well the group or team functioned to work toward its learning goals. Individual accountability (c) involves all individual student members taking responsibility for group or team success, hence being accountable for it. Positive interdependence (d) entails student group work or teamwork in assigned member roles to attain shared goals.

53. C: Claire's behavior suggests that she is influenced by media messaging which can have positive and negative effects. Excessive exercise often accompanies the eating disorder anorexia nervosa, but there are no signs of an eating disorder. Claire is obsessed with a celebrity and not a peer/friend/classmate, which would be peer pressure. Communities can also apply pressure to exercise, but Claire's behavior is not motivated by community members.

54. B: The integrated model best describes this approach that includes teaching other content areas to help foster holistic understanding. Quidditch, a fictional game in the Harry Potter series, is a game that was later developed for real-life physical education based on this approach. The tactical approach is used in team sports to develop decision-making skills. The cooperative games approach allows students to make choices on solving problems collectively. The skill themes approach focuses on skill development to foster skill competence and skill transfer across games and activities.

55. C: Bandura identified and described observational learning. Among factors influencing it, he included Attention (a), meaning students must observe the teacher or model; Retention (b), meaning students must encode and store movement patterns in memory for retrieval; Motor Reproduction (c), meaning students repeatedly practice the kinesthetic and neuromuscular patterns modeled until they can imitate them; and Incentives and Reinforcement (d), which motivate students to perform the others.

56. B: Elementary is the most appropriate school level to teach movement education as it is the foundation for the fundamental movements (locomotor and non-locomotor), movement concepts (spatial awareness, relationships, and effort), and the three domains of learning (psychomotor, cognitive, and affective). These foundational skills and concepts aid in progressive, mature movements taught in middle and high school needed for individual and team sports, as well as fitness activities. Some pre-kindergarten programs are included in elementary school physical education programs, while others are offered at daycare centers.

57. A: Partner activities focus on relationships with others. While leading and following are partner activities, these are under the "relationship with others" movement concept. Partner activities are the normal progression before participating in larger team activities but are not movement concepts. High and low levels can also be taught in pairs but are subcomponents of the movement concept spatial awareness.

58. D: The integumentary system is made up of the skin, hair, and nails and is responsible for excreting sweat from the skin. The primary purpose of perspiration is to aid in thermoregulation which cools down the body to protect it from overheating and warms up the body to protect it from cold-related conditions. The nervous system plays a part in sweating as well, as it is responsible for activating and regulating the sweat response. In physical activity responses, the parasympathetic nervous system is responsible for exciting the body and the sympathetic nervous system is responsible for calming the body down. The immune system is responsible for fighting off infections. The endocrine system includes the pancreas, thyroid, and pituitary and adrenal glands. The endocrine system is responsible for heart rate, blood pressure, bone and muscle mass increases, and glucose transportation to the muscles during physical activity.

59. D: Recently, the issue that has become the greatest challenge to kindergarten to Grade 12 (K–12) school physical education (PE) is that time in school curricula for PE classes and activities has been reduced significantly to make time for other academic classes. Inadequate resources and parental support (A); overly large class sizes and teacher burnout (B); and violence, student drug abuse, and discipline problems (C) are also challenges to K–12 PE, but these are also equal challenges to other school subjects and to education in general.

60. D: A sudden decline in academic performance could be caused by any of the factors listed. Certain eating disorders can cause declines in academic performance because of physical symptoms like lethargy and the students' attendant lack of motivation. Drug use can also cause lethargy, inattentiveness, and/or hyperactivity that can affect schoolwork. Parental divorce can cause depression and inability to focus, which can also contribute to a decline in academic achievement. However, it is important to remember that these problems do not always cause declines in academic achievement. Joining a sports team may cause sudden change in a student's life, causing them to need to adjust to perform well in both sporting and academic pursuits. Once the student is adjusted, participation in a school sports team should not cause problems with academics and, in fact, may reinforce study habits if the team requires the student to achieve a certain grade point average.

61. B: First aid procedures include RICE (rest, ice, compression, and elevation) to reduce inflammation. Immobilization restricts movement and further damage. Moving or mobilization (A) may cause more damage. Heat (C) is used for long-term musculoskeletal injuries but for new injuries or when in doubt, use ice. Heat can increase swelling and inflammation of new injuries. Calling 911 (D) is for life-threatening injuries. Sprains heal in time. Severe sprains and follow-up visits tend to occur with a primary care or orthopedic doctor.

62. D: Moving creatively to varied music rhythms using simple dance steps (A) is a movement skill competency suitable for students in the first grade. Jumping rope to the tempo of music, both singly and with a partner (B), is suitable for students in the second grade. Bouncing, passing, and catching a ball to match a musical rhythm (C) is suitable for students in the third grade. Expressing feelings or ideas through rhythmic motion, with and without music (D), is suitable for students in the fifth grade.

63. A: A chasse is a ballet step adopted in jazz and modern dance and is similar to the gallop where one foot leads and the other follows. An axel is a turn used in jazz and modern dance but consists of turning while hopping. The ball change is a transition step used in jazz that consists of transferring weight on the balls of the feet, similar to the weight transfer that occurs in the grapevine step. The drop is an intentional fall to the ground, often after performing a leap.

64. D: The teacher should take attendance before and after the hike to ensure that all students are present, as people can get lost on hiking trails. Applying sunscreen and having a charged cell phone are important safety factors. School leadership and the physical education team should be given advance notice that students are being taken out for a hike. Student-leaders can be helpful but are not a procedural practice.

65. B: Setting team goals fosters teamwork since, ideally, all members agree and are committed to working towards the same goal. Team captains help lead and can remind players of the common goals, but this is not the best strategy to foster teamwork, as not all teams have captains. Meeting with players individually is more appropriate for individual goal setting or to inform players of behaviors counter to teamwork, such as not passing the ball. Watching videos can help identify and provide feedback regarding teamwork, but setting goals and expectations must occur for this to be an effective strategy.

66. B: Given John's free throw-shooting ability, his performance was negatively impacted due to individual and environmental constraints. Individual constraints include structural constraints (e.g., height, body size, and gender) and functional constraints (cognitive and psychological issues, including arousal). Spectators, fans, and different noises occur during game play, which is a different environment than the practice environment. John is also playing against opponents instead of teammates, which is also an environmental constraint. As such, these environmental constraints are having negative impacts on John's performance.

67. A: While offensive and defensive skills are evident in basketball, tennis, and floor hockey, manipulative skills best describe the use of motor skills, which encompasses offensive and defensive movements. Manipulative skills are advanced fundamental movement skills that combine locomotor and non-locomotor skills and include fine and gross muscle movements while using equipment. Skills performed in team and dual sports are open skills, as the environment is unpredictable.

68. C: The President's Council on Physical Fitness and Sports identifies "Fundamental Building Blocks" for using PE to promote positive student development. The structure of these is that giving opportunities and access to PA for all young people enables establishing ideal contexts for engaging in PA, which in turn allows PE educators to help students attain developmental health outcomes.

69. C: Training at a percentage of the maximum heart rate (MHR) is used to assess heart rate intensity during exercise. For cardiovascular fitness, working at 65 to 85% of the MHR is the recommended range, with beginners starting at the lower limits and advanced exercisers working at the upper limits. Elite endurance athletes or those with high cardiovascular fitness can work at 90% of MHR. Continuous aerobic activity is a method to determine the time and/or distance of the activity. The talk test aids in determining relative intensity based on if one can or cannot talk or sing during cardiovascular activities. If one is unable to talk, the intensity is too high for continuous activity. If one can talk but not sing, the intensity is at a moderate level. If they can sing, the intensity is too low. Recovery heart rate is the time it takes for the heart to return to normal or rest after activity and is one way to measure cardiovascular improvements. The fitter one becomes, the faster the heart rate returns to normal.

70. B: Skill circuit variation can aid in skill development and refinement to meet diverse learners or mixed-ability groups. All students can work on the same skills but are challenged according to their ability. For example, in a shooting circuit, beginner students can work on technique closer to the basketball goal, intermediate students can shoot mid-range, and advanced students can shoot at farther distances at the same circuit. While student choice has been shown to increase motivation, students may not necessarily choose tasks that match or improve their ability. Combining mixed-ability or pairing advanced and beginner students is appropriate in some settings, e.g., peer assessment, but advanced and beginner students can become frustrated, so progress may suffer at both ends of the ability continuum. Beginner students may also get injured by intermediate and advance students, especially during gameplay activities.

71. A: The self-determination theory is a psychological approach used to teach physical education to increase intrinsic student motivation by providing students with achievable but challenging tasks. Intrinsic motivation has shown most effective in fostering appreciation and lifelong physical activity engagement. Behaviorism focuses on the psychomotor domain and is a teacher-directed approach that works to change students' behaviors based on the environment the teacher creates. Social theory relies heavily on the affective domain, or the social aspects of student engagement, and underpins cooperative and sport education models where students work together to solve problems. Constructivism theory focuses on the cognitive domain and works toward providing students with an understanding of what they are doing and why in the psychomotor and affective domains.

72. C: The purpose of assessment in physical education is to measure student learning. If learning is not measured, the teacher will not know their students' level of education or what they are capable of. Teachers reflect on lesson plans to ensure that activities are working towards the objectives, thus fostering learning. Objectives are the outcomes or desired goals, but the assessment is done to measure the learning of the objectives.

73. A: The Institute of Medicine recommendation is for children to spend an hour a day in moderate to vigorous physical activity (MVPA). But studies show that, in actual schools, physical education (PE) classes last about 23 minutes a day, with only 10 of those minutes spent in MVPA. In other words, children get about one-sixth the MVPA that is recommended from school PE classes. Researchers conclude that not only must children be physically active outside of PE classes, but also schools must increase how much children are active during PE class times.

74. A: Students need more extrinsic (external) feedback from teachers or coaches when learning new PE skills. When they are more competent and confident with certain PE skills, they can analyze their own performance and make use of this intrinsic (internal) feedback. Choice (b) has this backwards. Students need both positive feedback for reinforcement and encouragement and negative feedback for correction (c), and both constructive and corrective (d) feedback, at all learning stages.

75. B: Respiratory syncytial virus (RSV) is a very common childhood illness, though many are unfamiliar with its name. Symptoms are similar enough to common colds and flu that one may not know the difference without diagnosis. It can also be contracted at any age; most people are exposed to it by the age of 2 years. After having it a few times, most people simply regard it as a cold. However, experts say RSV is not only more common in children, but also causes children more problems than flu. Fifth disease, due to human parvovirus, can cause rashes and cold-like symptoms; however, many children show *no* symptoms, and it is typically *not* serious (A). Human hand, foot, and mouth disease *is* common in childhood, caused by *viruses*, and typically *not* serious (C), though it can cause considerable discomfort for 7–10 days. While about 6% of young children do get croup annually, only up to 6% of these are hospitalized, and children very seldom die of croup (D).

76. B: Younger children have difficulty tracking objects visually, which negatively impacts hand-eye coordination. Using a larger ball increases the surface area or points of contact, which makes it easier to see and strike. Striking a ball while it is airborne is a more difficult task because it requires a faster reaction time and is a skill used for more advanced students. Moving closer to the net would be used if the student could not get the ball over the net. Early preparation ensures earlier contact rather than late, which helps with the direction of the ball.

77. A: The bowler should use a heavier ball for more power to knock down all of the pins. There is no need for the bowler to move left since the middle pin is struck consistently. Putting more spin on the ball would help the bowler achieve a strike if the pins were struck from the side rather than down the middle. The bowler will likely lose power if the ball is thrown from farther away.

78. C: Jumping fast and landing softly illustrate the movement concept of effort, which includes time and force. Tempo refers to the speed or timing of the movement (jumping fast), and force refers to how hard or softly the movement is performed (landing softly). Strong and weak are cues or terms used for emphasis or to describe the movement concepts, but these terms are ambiguous (e.g., the bodybuilder was strong; the illness made her weak) and do not clearly convey the movement concept of effort.

79. B: Proprioceptive neuromuscular facilitation (PNF) has been shown to have the most significant improvements for flexibility. It consists of variations of the four types of stretches with a contraction-relaxation pattern. Active stretching is typically an unassisted static stretch where the individual provides the force of the stretch, e.g., quad stretch. Passive stretching is an assisted stretch where someone or an object aids in deepening the stretch. Both active and passive stretching can be static or dynamic. Dynamic stretches are performed with movement and preferred for warm-ups for secondary-aged students. Ballistic stretches are bouncy or jerky and should be avoided to reduce the risk of overstretching or other injury.

80. C: Hyperthermia is a significant increase in body temperature, which increases the risks of heat exhaustion, heat stroke, and death. Hypothermia is a significant decrease in the body's temperature, which can occur when training in extreme cold temperatures and can also lead to death. Physical activity engagement under normal conditions increases heart rate and sweat production. When the body loses the ability to sweat, the risk of hyperthermia increases.

81. A: According to social psychologists, nonverbal communication has these primary functions: performing social rituals (choice A), revealing personalities as well as interpersonal relationships, supporting verbal interactions, and expressing feelings. Choices B, C, and D are incorrect because they wrongly deny or limit these functions.

82. B: Female students can get stronger but will not achieve increased muscle mass on their own since the female body produces smaller amounts of testosterone, the dominant male hormone responsible for building and increasing muscle mass. Adolescent males will also have difficulty increasing muscle mass because physiological adaptations of size tend to occur after puberty ceases. Bodyweight exercises are good options when free weights are not available and both are utilized to increase muscular fitness, but without a significant amount of testosterone or growth hormone, female students are not likely to develop large muscles. Free weights are also appropriate for women and girls. A significant increase in nutrient intake can lead to fat weight gain but an increase in nutrient intake alone will not aid in increased musculature. Partnering students with similar goals may be beneficial but this partnership will not likely dispel the myth that female students will look more masculine if they participate in weight training.

83. C: Tracy should pinch her nose with the index finger and thumb while breathing through the mouth to stop the bleeding. The bleeding will worsen if she blows her nose. Tilting or holding her head back can cause blood to pool in the back of the throat and cause vomiting. A pair of gloves would be required for others who would be in contact with any student's blood to reduce potential disease transmission risk. If the bleeding does not stop within a few minutes, she should be sent to the nurse.

84. D: The Centers for Disease Control and Prevention (CDC) and SHAPE America recommend that children engage in an accumulated 60 minutes of cardiovascular activities every day, and the CDC recommends adults engage in 30 minutes of cardiovascular activities a day or 150-300 minutes a week to prevent cardiovascular risks (hypertension, heart disease, obesity) and maintain a healthy body weight.

85. A: Exercise depletes the muscles' glycogen stores, so within the first 30 minutes to two hours after exercising, participants should eat or drink simple carbohydrates while muscles absorb them better. Students and others with inadequate diets may need vitamin-mineral supplements, but with balanced nutrition, these are generally unnecessary (b). Although adequate daily hydration is critical in both everyday activities and exercise, it is a myth that everybody needs eight glasses a day (c): amount of fluid loss determines amount of water needed. Vitamins do not supply energy (d); they help release chemical energy from foods.

86. A: FITT = Frequency, Intensity, Time, Type. How long to work out (A) = Time, which is determined by the Intensity and Type of exercise. How to ensure overload without overtraining (B), burnout, or injury = Intensity. How often to work out to ensure enough stress to make the body adapt plus allow healing through enough rest (C) = Frequency. Specific exercises to do, and whether the workout is cardio, resistance (weight), or both combined (D) = Type.

87. A: Variable practice has shown most effective for team sports, as there is a lot of variability that occurs during game play. Variable practice provides random stimuli to help the body and mind prepare for any situation. Massed practice involves long practice sessions with little rest. Although it may build conditioning, the associated fatigue can reduce learning quality compared with distributed or variable practice, even if the practice content itself can be varied or consistent. Distributed practices are mini-practice sessions over a long period of time.

88. B: Research-based strategies found to promote student motivation include not only teacher interest in student learning, but also teacher personal interest (A) in their students' backgrounds and concerns; teacher demonstration of their own motivation and passion as role models for students (B); teacher belief in students' abilities (C) as well as interest in students; and teacher personalization of content for individual students (D).

89. D: Body weight training (c) uses no equipment, just the student's own body weight, for resistance. Partner resistance exercises (b) also require no equipment, just two students taking turns providing and working against resistance. Free weight work (a) can use dumbbells, kettlebells, etc., of different weights, or barbells to which weights can be added and subtracted; this requires equipment, but not the number or variety included in circuit training (d), which involves completing circuits through a series of different weight machines quickly without interruption.

90. A: The student has medical clearance to engage in physical education, which includes physical activity engagement. The teacher should provide low-impact activities that do not involve jumping, which puts additional stress on the knee joints. Allowing the student to choose from a list of exercises without jumps is appropriate, but not from a generic list or range of exercises because they may not have the knowledge of exercises that promote or impede a full recovery.

91. D: Squats with added weight promote quadriceps strength. Abductors are in the outer thigh area, and the quadriceps are in the front of the thigh. Bridges work the gluteus maximus, and deadlifts work the hamstrings and lower back.

92. B: The deltoids are the muscles of the shoulders and consist of posterior, lateral, and anterior. Lateral deltoid raises best train the shoulders from the exercise options. Lat pulls train the latissimus dorsi in the upper back. Overhead triceps train the back of the upper arm, and shrugs train the trapezius muscles that are connected to the deltoids.

93. D: Maximum heart rate is calculated by subtracting age from 220; e.g., for a 14-year-old student, 220-14 = 206 beats per minute (bpm). The target heart rate zone is 65-85 percent of maximum; 50-65 percent (a) is recommended for people unaccustomed to exercising or very out of shape; 85-100 percent (b) is a high-intensity zone recommended for athletes and other highly fit individuals; and 50 percent or less (c) is the zone for warming up and cooling down before and after exercise.

94. D: The Teaching Personal and Social Responsibility (TPSR) helps students navigate the positives and negatives in life in physical education settings, including success, failure, challenge, and perseverance, that aid in the development of self-evaluation and monitoring. TPSR is designed to teach personal and social skills and help students manage their behaviors in and out of school. Cooperative learning requires students to work together to solve a problem independently of the teacher. Guided-discovery is a type of cooperative learning where the teacher guides students by posing questions or prompts that help them meet the objective. Social Emotional Learning (SEL) focuses on the affective domain and is designed to ensure a safe and equitable environment for all students.

95. C: Mr. Green can reduce the time it takes for attendance by taking it when students are engaged in an activity like the warm-up or instant activity. Setting an attendance time-limit will not likely decrease the time as 40 students need to be accounted for. Mr. Green could practice but practicing a managerial tool takes away from planning for instruction/learning. Squad lines where students sit or stand in the same spot make it easier to see absent students but unless a warm-up or activity is conducted in the squad lines, students have to wait to be engaged in activities.

96. B: Of the activities named, swimming is ideal for students with joint problems because it puts no weight or stress on the joints. The buoyancy of the body in water keeps weight and impact off the joints. Students can be active and get exercise without aggravating joint conditions or pain. Skiing (A) requires a lot of knee bending and turning, hip swiveling, and bearing weight on the joints, so it is not compatible with joint problems. Skateboarding (C) also involves much knee bending and turning, as well as jumping and landing, and would be hard on joint problems. Playing soccer (D) requires running and kicking, again putting too much impact on the joints. These other sports also are done on the ground and subject to gravity, whereas swimming relieves the joints of weight.

97. D: Beginning students make lots of errors and focus heavily on skill cues, so the teacher needs to be intentional and direct with instruction to help the student understand the movements of the skill. As students begin to understand the movement as illustrated in improvement, the need for direct feedback and demonstrations are reduced.

98. B: The size of the heart increases from consistent participation in cardiovascular activities. The body becomes more reliant on glucose to faster fuel the working muscles. Blood volume also increases as a result of the heart's strengthening which allows for more blood to circulate. Lactic acid removal is more efficient, allowing for a faster recovery.

99. B: Non-competitive collaboration best describes cooperative learning. Students work together to solve various outcomes based on students' decisions rather than pre-determined outcomes, as with competitive sports and teacher-driven outcomes. Peer and group activities occur in cooperative learning but also occur in all other teaching approaches.

100. B: The Heimlich maneuver should be performed only on someone who is choking and cannot breathe. This means the person cannot speak, so the Heimlich maneuver should not be performed on a student who says he or she is having trouble breathing. Someone who is choking and cannot breathe also cannot cough, so the Heimlich maneuver should not be performed on a student who is coughing, which means he or she can breathe. The Heimlich maneuver should be done first if someone is choking; cardiopulmonary resuscitation (CPR) should be started after that if the victim loses consciousness.

101. D: Protecting students' safety both within and outside of the classroom requires that educators are aware of how to recognize and address signs of child abuse or neglect. Children that are being abused or neglected in the home may display a sudden change in behavior in class. These students may become hostile, easily agitated, or disruptive. Other indicators include a decline in the students' grades, withdrawal, and poor hygiene practices. Upon observing these signs, it is important that teachers report their suspicions to child protective services immediately and follow the policies outlined in their district's professional code of conduct regarding procedures for reporting child abuse or neglect.

102. A: Heart rate monitors detect the speed or rate that the heart beats and determines exercise intensity. An accelerometer is a tracking device that can inform the teacher of students' acceleration or speed changes since acceleration is a change in speed. Pedometers are step counters that track the number of steps taken. Some fitness tracking devices include all of the above as well as sleep, sitting, and minutes engaged in physical activity.

103. C: Students engage in walking, jogging, and running when engaged in orienteering. In a triathlon, fitness activities include swimming, cycling, and running or jogging. Hiking, swimming, and cycling benefit muscular and cardiovascular fitness but are not skills used in orienteering.

104. A: Eating a high carbohydrate meal, also known as carb loading, before an endurance activity is done for fast and easy recruitment of glucose and glycogen energy rather than waiting 20-minutes for the fat energy stores to become available, which could slow down a runner's pace. If running on an empty stomach, the body will need to recruit stored glucose (glycogen). While glycogen is a faster energy source than fats, glucose obtained from a light snack or breakfast is more ideal as it is already in the bloodstream and does not need to metabolize or be broken down like glycogen and stored fat. The meal is equitable but that is not the most important reason for eating a high carbohydrate meal before an endurance activity. Depending on the time the meal is eaten, it may help or hurt sleep, but it is not the purpose of carb loading.

105. B: Zigzag running or alternating diagonal patterns are common in dual and team sports. Transitions occur in dual and team sports, but it is the transition from offense to defense and vice versa with footwork patterns differing across sport types. Curve patterns are not common in dual and team sports. Some team sports have high-level movements like jumping in volleyball and basketball, but dual sports such as tennis and badminton, use mostly medium-level movements but not defensive running patterns.

106. B: As students enter adolescence, their social lives will most likely revolve around membership in a small social group that has a shared set of values and interests. While students maintain interest in family, they will increasingly choose to spend more time with friends. While violence is likely to affect the lives of some students, physical insecurity is not a predominant characteristic of most adolescents. Adolescents also begin to show an increased interest in their ethnic or cultural heritage as part of the identity-formation process.

107. B: The principle of overload best explains Blake's soreness, as he exercised too hard and too fast after not engaging in a workout for three months. Blake should have engaged in progressive overload, which is the gradual increase in intensity, rather than engaging at full effort right from the start. Without knowledge of Blake's previous fitness levels, there is not enough information to determine if Blake regressed or reverted back to his fitness status three months prior.

108. D: FITT = Frequency, Intensity, Time, Type. Overload increases fitness by increasing workload so the body adapts and can do more. Increasing number of workout days increases Frequency for BOTH resistance AND cardio training. Different exercise (A) changes Type for cardio training; for resistance training, this would involve different exercises BUT the same body area. Increasing repetitions (B) increases Time for resistance training; for cardio, one would increase duration. Increasing resistance (C) increases Intensity for weight training; for cardio, one would increase pace or percentage of maximum heartrate.

109. D: The mildest form of heat illness is dehydration (C), caused by fluid loss through perspiration. Exercising too long in the heat causes greater fluid loss and also salt loss, which can cause heat cramps (B), the next mildest form. If one continues exertion after experiencing dehydration or heat cramp symptoms, this can lead to more serious heat exhaustion (A). Intense exertion in the heat can make the body produce more heat than it can release, resulting in heat stroke (D), the most severe form.

110. C: Skill isolation is appropriate when learning or developing a new skill. Practicing skills in isolation slows down the pace. As skills gradually improve, the challenge should increase, like incorporating speed, a defender, and engaging in small-sided games. While most physical education programs are co-ed, research shows that girls engage in more physical activity and are more skillful in same-gender PE programs; however, isolation of skills would still occur in same-gendered classes. A "touch" will likely not lead to proficiency in ball-handling skills because the opportunities to develop are limited.

111. A: Katherine is aware of her performance, showing that she has knowledge of performance, which is a type of intrinsic feedback used to detect and correct movement skills errors. Knowledge of performance becomes more effective in advanced performers who know why they performed the way they did and are less reliant on teachers and coaches to tell them what went wrong and how to correct it. Knowledge of results is the knowledge of the performance outcome, which is a type of extrinsic feedback. Katherine's throw likely went in the direction that her body rotated, which she would be able to see after the ball lands, which is also terminal feedback or feedback that occurs at the end, which can correct errors. Positive transfer is when skills used in one activity, e.g., serving in volleyball, promotes skill performance in another activity, such as serving in tennis. Negative transfer is when skills used in one activity impedes skill performance in another.

112. A: A dynamic warm-up is a safe practice for dance and other physical activities to prepare the body for vigorous work and prevent injury. Static movements or stationary stretching should occur at the end of the activity as stretching a cold muscle increases the risks of muscle tears and blood pools to the muscle stretched instead of throughout the body to all muscles used. Wearing loose clothing may be more comfortable but generally is not considered a safety precaution. Yoga stretches and poses consist of many static movements or stretches held for long periods, which restricts blood flow from circulation to all the muscles.

113. D: White blood cell production, also known as leukocytes, occurs in the bone marrow. Because leukocytes are central to immune function, bone marrow is considered part of the lymphatic system. Bone marrow is also considered part of the skeletal system, but since this is not an answer choice, lymphatic is the best option. The lymphatic system is a major part of the immune system, as is it responsible for the development, maturation, and circulation of immune cells. The integumentary system refers to the skin and other external features of the body. The nervous system connects the brain with the muscles and senses. It is responsible for many bodily functions, but it is not related to white blood cells. The circulatory system is responsible for pumping blood and nutrients throughout the body.

114. A: When teammates get along, it is easier for them to accomplish team goals (e.g., scoring, winning). Teammates that do not get along impede team success. Strategies that help build teamwork include designing small goals that the team can accomplish together and gradually increasing these tasks. Trust activities also help foster teamwork. The coach should also communicate to players team changes and the rationale behind those changes to diffuse any animosity between players.

115. D: Teachers can give students cards with adverbs they recently learned, have them look up synonyms and antonyms for these, and write them on the cards. The teacher then directs the students to perform movements in ways described by the adverbs on their cards. The teacher then has students pass their cards to classmates and repeat the activity with new words. This lesson integrates physical education (PE) and English language arts (ELA) skills. Performing movements and then working with words separately or vice versa (options A and B) does not integrate PE and ELA skills together into the same activity. Describing movements using the adverbs (C) makes a mental connection between words and movement, but the students are not actually performing any body movements; they are only describing them verbally, so this is an ELA activity rather than an integrated PE and ELA activity.

116. C: Landing with soft or bent knees allows the body to absorb a fall's shock or reduce the amount of force applied to the body, thus reducing injury or the likelihood of injury. Locked knees can cause the joints to hyperextend, which increases the risk of bone and muscle injuries. The spacing of the feet is determined by the activity. For instance, the feet are close together while jumping rope but shoulder-distance apart during a jump squat.

117. A: Experts at PE Central say one way PE teachers can create a positive climate for student activity and learning is to increase the opportunities for students to learn. They also say creating this positive climate requires using many varied motivational strategies (b), helping students learn and sustain appropriate behaviors (c), and promoting student responsibility and accountability (d).

118. B: Skeletal muscles are responsible for muscle contraction and voluntary movements. The sliding filament theory (D) is the widely accepted theory that explains the process of concentric muscular contractions. Smooth muscles (A) are involuntary and responsible for intestinal contractions to help transport food throughout the body. Cardiac muscles (C) are also involuntary and are muscles of the heart responsible for contractions in the heart.

119. C: Stephanie ignored the progression principle, which is the gradual increase in overload when beginning a workout routine. Stephanie engaged in overload or engaged in activities greater than normal but did too much. Specificity is engaging in activities that support the goal. For example, if the goal is to run the mile faster, running fast needs to be a part of the workout or training program.

120. C: Using a stopwatch or clock timer is an appropriate measure of duration or time engaged in aerobic activities for large classes. Pedometers are quick, easy, low-tech activity trackers that measure step count but do not measure duration (B). Pedometers and other activity trackers, e.g., Fitbits or Polar HR monitors, can waste instructional time and be expensive (A). There also may not be enough pedometers or activity trackers to use for large classes. Aerobic equipment, including treadmills, ellipticals, cycles, and rowing machines have timers; however, there usually are not enough for all students to use simultaneously(D).

121. D: ESSA, or the Every Student Succeeds Act, recognizes the value that health and physical education have on developing the whole child. Parents should also be informed that physical education is not just fun and games but a way of learning psychomotor, cognitive, affective, and social domains. Title IX is the law that guarantees equal educational and athletic access to all genders. SHAPE America's toolkit is a resource that teachers can use in their instructional planning. IDEA is the Individuals with Disabilities Education Act that guarantees a quality educational experience for students with disabilities.

122. C: Factors that can often prevent diverse parents and families from communicating and participating in the education of their children include language barriers, which frequently stop them from communicating (A); unsuccessful parent school histories, which can make them feel ineffectual to participate (B); feeling alienated from school processes because of their differing cultures (C) and/or languages; and poor past experiences with schools, which can make them reluctant to participate (D).

123. D: Progressive partner-resistance exercises (aka partner-assisted manual resistance) allows for better isolation of the muscle trained, as the partner is able to apply greater resistance or additional overload when weights are not available—a good option for PE programs that have little to no resistance training equipment. Students need to be trained prior to attempting this exercise because it is a type of training that can increase the risk of injury. Communication is critical to inform the partner when there is too much resistance applied and when more resistance is required.

124. A: Novice learners need visual and verbal instructions (skill cues) of the skills they are expected to perform. If there is too much variation in the task, the novice will miss critical elements of the pitch. For improvement and mastery, activities that the learner engages in should be directly related to the skill/task objectives and goals.

125. A: Research has found that frequent teacher praise encourages students (A) to want to learn. Teacher praise should be frequent and offered freely to encourage students, and being too judicious with praise should be avoided, as praise should be given for all student effort (B). This type of freely offered praise promotes rather than inhibits self-motivation (C). While negatively oriented criticism might discourage students, constructive criticism from teachers does not (D); it encourages them and promotes self-motivation.

126. D: Small-sided games are modified versions of games that allow for more opportunities to respond. Instead of five vs. five basketball, implementing two vs. two or three vs. three games increases student opportunity to integrate manipulative skills. Choice is a strategy used to increase student motivation. Leading and following can be used for isolation skills but do not foster integration in game-like situations. Mirroring works best with locomotor and non-locomotor movements. Demonstrations are more useful for refinement and integration of manipulative skills.

127. A: The Presidential Youth Fitness and FitnessGram® programs are designed to assess health-related fitness, including muscular endurance, muscular strength, cardiovascular endurance, flexibility, and body composition, as these components impact life quality. Skill-related fitness (B) is sport-related or performance skills and includes power, agility, coordination, speed, reaction time, and balance. Fitness assessments that measure both skills- and health-related fitness (C) are assessments used for military entry and training, including the candidate fitness test. Dynamic and non-dynamic or static activities (D) are conducted in the Presidential Youth and FitnessGram® assessments but do not include sports skills.

128. B: Back extensions will help with posture by increasing flexibility in the lower back, which causes the shoulders to pull back to an upright position. Kyphosis is an age-related hunched back condition that generally occurs in older women and differs from the hunched back postures among some students. Curl-ups may further the rounded or hunched back posture. A counter-balance exercise including push-ups would aid in posture corrections. The pec deck may also aid in the rounding of shoulders and back. A counter-balance exercise including rear delts would help with posture.

129. D: Self-efficacy is the personal belief of accomplishment in motor skills and performance. As players become more competent in skill and game performance, their self-efficacy tends to increase. Because there is no one else to rely on during individual sports, athletes must be able to self-motivate and self-correct.

130. C: Fitbit devices can help physical education teachers to support and increase student motivation and also include a line of designer fashion accessories. They can be used for both controlling weight and monitoring sleep quality (A). Students can self-monitor their own progress using Fitbit devices; they also can use them to challenge and compete with friends (B). They are not just stand-alone progress trackers (D); they also sync wirelessly with mobile smartphones and tablets and with charts, graphs, and badges available online for documenting improvements and gaining insights about physical fitness.

Practice Test #2

1. Which of the following should be a part of a school's emergency plan?

a. First aid kit
b. Exit routes
c. Student medications
d. Lesson plans

2. Which of the following is a kinesthetic skill improvement technique used in physical education?

a. the sandwich method
b. knowledge of results
c. video analysis
d. knowledge of feedback

3. Which of the following PE activities demonstrates motor or movement skills that a typically developing student should be able to perform by the end of the third grade?

a. Using a bat to hit a ball pitched by another
b. Catch, dribble, pass ball to moving partner
c. Jumping a rope while others are twirling it
d. Jumping a rope that one is twirling oneself

4. Of the following, which best describes high school learning standards for balance skills in PE?

a. Utilizing dynamic balance for transitions in gymnastics, between sport movements
b. Creating and showing a balance sequence using counterbalances, counter-tensions
c. Demonstrating a variety of static and dynamic balance, either singly or with others
d. Demonstrating static balance with different body parts, shapes, and support bases

5. In a PE class, which of these would be an example of descriptive feedback?

a. "Wow, great form!"
b. "Stand sideways!"
c. "Use your instep!"
d. "Follow through!"

6. When designing, choosing, modifying, and sequencing game activities, what should PE teachers have as their main purpose(s)?

a. To ensure that students remain occupied
b. To enhance skills practice and enjoyment
c. To ensure student behavior management
d. To enhance student enjoyment primarily

7. At the beginning of the semester, a student had a resting heart rate of 72 bpm, and by the end of the unit, the resting heart rate was 82 bpm. Which of the following best explains the change in heart rate?

a. An increase in fitness
b. A decrease in fitness
c. Heart disease
d. Tachycardia

8. Which of the following laws or guidelines protects students' medical and personal information?

a. HIPAA
b. IDEA
c. ADHD
d. FERPA

9. Why are variation and goal setting important in physical education?

a. To minimize student complaints
b. To aid in curriculum development
c. To adhere to district guidelines
d. To promote interest and engagement

10. Which of the following agencies sets the national K-12 physical education standards?

a. CAEP
b. GOPHER
c. NASPE
d. SHAPE

11. Which of the following is an example of metabolic syndrome related to sedentary lifestyles?

a. Heart disease and overactive thyroid
b. High cholesterol, hypertension, and obesity
c. Hypokinetic disease and physical inactivity
d. Obesity, low blood glucose, and diabetes

12. A teacher is preparing for the invasion games unit in which last year's students struggled with decision-making during game play. Which instructional approach or model is most appropriate to help students with the decision-making process?

a. Sport Education Model
b. Tactical games approach
c. Direct teaching approach
d. Cooperative learning approach

13. Which of the following is a strategy used to develop locomotor and non-locomotor movements?

a. games
b. equipment
c. choice
d. mirroring

14. Which of the following practice styles has been shown to be the most effective in improving student performance in PE and sport settings?

a. Random practice
b. Variable practice
c. Blocked practice
d. Mental practice

15. Which of the following is a risk of engaging in cardiovascular endurance training in the cold?

a. hypothermia
b. hyperthermia
c. vasodilation
d. getting a cold

16. Which of these is an effective strategy for physical education teachers to enhance students' perceived physical competence?

a. Specify the number of trials to complete during a certain time period.
b. Specify the length of time for practicing but not the number of trials.
c. Specify the technical errors students make in instructional feedback.
d. Specify a certain activity without varying it to keep students on task.

17. Which of the following is an example of a SHAPE America grade level outcome?

a. The student will recognize value in physical activity
b. The student will demonstrate motor skills
c. The student will apply movement concepts
d. The student will skip using a mature pattern

18. Which of the following is a good explanation of why several students throughout the school year have contracted bacterial infections after physical education classes?

a. coughing with their mouths open
b. engaging in skin-to-skin contact
c. rolling around on mats
d. failing to shower after class

19. Which of the following agencies set the goals and curricula for state-level K-12 physical education?

a. SHAPE
b. CAEP
c. HPE
d. ESSA

20. Which one of the following statements about objectives is *not* true?

a. Objectives are a communications tool aimed specifically at the students, not other audiences.
b. Objectives provide a way to evaluate student learning.
c. Objectives help focus and motivate students.
d. Objectives provide a way for teachers to measure their own effectiveness.

Refer to the following for question 21:

High school students in a physical education class are beginning an outdoor unit on tennis. During the first session, the teacher notices that some students are struggling to get the ball over the net during the forehand stroke. Later on in the week, the teacher notices that one student, Ari, is constantly having her tennis ball land beyond the baseline (out of bounds or longer) during her tennis forehand.

21. Which of the following is an appropriate modification for students who struggle to get the ball over the net during the forehand stroke?

a. Lowering the net
b. Practicing against a wall
c. Getting closer to the net
d. Watching a peer demonstrate the forehand

22. Among the following common areas of negligence in physical education, in addition to first aid emergencies, which one can teachers and coaches MOST mitigate by enlisting the help of students?

a. Instruction
b. Supervision
c. Transportation
d. Class environments

23. Which level is primarily responsible for the initial development of K-12 physical education standards in the United States of America?

a. National organizations
b. State education agencies
c. Physical education teachers
d. School districts

24. Where should a sprinter's center of gravity be to accelerate fastest out of the starting block?

a. It should be as high as possible.
b. It should be as low as possible.
c. It should be right in the middle.
d. It should be a full upright body.

25. Students have physical education two days a week and are not meeting physical activity recommendations. Which of the following are realistic community resources that provide physical activity opportunities for all students?

a. parks and recreation
b. hiking trails
c. rock climbing
d. fitness centers

26. Regarding appropriate physical education (PE) teaching practices, which statement is most valid?

a. PE teachers must use extrinsic motivations to teach students responsibility for learning.
b. PE teachers should ignore certain inappropriate student behaviors to extinguish them.
c. PE teachers do not necessarily need to obtain or renew certification in cardiopulmonary resuscitation (CPR) or automated external defibrillator (AED) use.
d. PE teachers must regularly and consistently inspect facilities and equipment for safety.

27. When does physical education instruction necessarily require giving feedback to students?

a. When a skill requires specific correction
b. When a skill gets environmental feedback
c. When a student has experience with a skill
d. When a teacher can comprehensively demonstrate a skill

28. A spectator passes out during the football game and the CPR certified PE teacher is called to help. Which of the following steps should the PE teacher do first?

a. call 911
b. check the scene
c. check for breathing
d. start CPR

29. Which of the following is a common defensive strategy used during invasion games?

a. staying close to the opponent
b. V-cut or L-cut
c. a fake
d. getting open

30. Which of the following is the best reason for a self-assessment assignment?

a. To refine skills
b. To assess learning preference
c. To aid the teacher in the summative assessment
d. To practice the summative assessment

31. Which biomechanical principle is best illustrated during the arched position of the Fosbury Flop technique used during the high jump?

a. Force
b. Torque
c. Angular momentum
d. Projectile motion

32. Coach Wheelock refuses to let the girls on the school's basketball team play with the boys in physical education because he says the boys play too rough. Which of the following practices does Coach Wheelock exhibit?

a. Safety for injury prevention
b. Gender discrimination
c. Favoritism towards the boys
d. Gender stereotypes

33. Which of the following is a proactive measure to reduce risks of injuries in physical education?

a. Locating the exit doors
b. Engaging in a warm-up
c. Contacting the principal in the event of an emergency
d. Assigning students to set up and break down equipment

34. Which of the following is NOT a minimum necessary feature of a school-wide emergency response plan?

a. Policies for emergency notification of parents and guardians
b. Floor plans and maps of the school
c. Establishment of communication systems
d. An on-site police officer

35. Which of the following is required equipment for fencing?

a. a singlet
b. a pair of shin guards
c. a foil
d. a large mat

36. The MyFitnessPal, Endomondo, and Fitbit digital fitness apps all share which feature?

a. Sync with devices or other fitness platforms
b. Built-in recipe databases
c. Real-time audio coaching during workouts
d. Guided workout video library

37. One student has an unusually short stature and has a difficult time getting the shuttlecock over the net during their serve. Which of the following is an equitable solution to this issue?

a. moving the student closer to the net
b. allowing the student's partner to serve
c. providing a box for the student to stand on
d. lowering the net

38. Which of the following helps students build confidence to perform a skill?

a. Skill cues
b. Competitive activities
c. Watching others
d. Critical self-talk

39. The teacher has little time to go over each health-related fitness component in isolation. Which of the following activities can the teacher use to implement the health-related fitness components when short on time?

a. resistance training
b. interval training
c. fartlek training
d. circuit training

40. Daniel received doctor's orders to strengthen his lower back before engaging in any other activities. Which of the following exercises will help him get stronger in the lower back?

a. lat pulls
b. one-arm rows
c. seated rows
d. trunk lifts

41. In general, when demonstrating PE skills or skill combinations, which principle applies most?

a. Demonstrate the skill as whole-part-whole.
b. Demonstrate only a skill's component parts.
c. Demonstrate the entire skill only as a whole.
d. Demonstrate by giving more, not fewer, cues.

42. Students and others who are obese, or are overweight and have two or more other risk factors, can decrease their risk of developing related diseases by losing how much of their existing body weight?

a. 5-10 percent
b. 15-20 percent
c. 25-30 percent
d. 35-40 percent

43. Which statement best characterizes the role of posture in theories of motor development?

a. As evidence of growing cerebral control, posture was more important to classical theories.
b. As the biomechanical basis of action, posture is more important to contemporary theories.
c. For different reasons, posture has been equally important to both earlier and later theories.
d. In both classical and contemporary theories, posture is a minor part of motor development.

44. Which of the following most significantly contributes to the growing problem of childhood obesity?

a. Cultural background
b. Socioeconomic status
c. Lifestyle factors
d. Genetic history

45. Which of the following exercises best work the trunk and quadriceps?

a. Curl-ups and deadlifts
b. Knee lifts and seated rows
c. Planks and squats
d. Twists and leg curls

46. A student is feeling anxious about an upcoming fitness test because he feels like he is going to be the slowest and weakest in his class. Which of the following types of stress best describes the anxiety the student is experiencing?

a. Eustress
b. Distress
c. Physical stress
d. Fight or flight stress

47. Mr. Jackson is excited to try out new teambuilding activities that he learned during the physical education professional development. Which strategy would MOST directly foster teamwork during a team-building activity?

a. Trust falls
b. Taking turns
c. Allowing students to pick teams
d. Rotating team captains

48. A student consistently engages in low-intensity cardiovascular activities during class and has low performance on the cardiovascular assessments. Which of the following recommendations may help this student increase intensity and improve?

a. Interval training with heart rate tracking
b. Using a pedometer with step count goal
c. Listing the benefits of cardiovascular health
d. Engaging in activity for longer periods of time

49. Which of the following activities improve flexibility and posture?

a. isometric training
b. plank exercises
c. free weight training
d. running

50. Among social, emotional, environmental, and health factors that affect motor development and performance, which of the following is the *best* example of the impact of social factors?

a. A student's insecurities impede participation in physical activities.
b. Many students would rather play video games than physical ones.
c. Poor home living conditions limit a student's physical activity and fitness.
d. A student's illness or disability makes physical activity challenging.

51. Students in class have a cross country meet tomorrow. Which of the following recommendations will help students prepare?

a. "Take a practice run on the course."
b. "Take a practice run at a lower intensity."
c. "Get more rest and increase fat intake."
d. "Get more rest and increase carbohydrate intake."

52. In addition to physical activity, which of the following activities has been shown to help manage stress?

a. Drinking red wine
b. Getting adequate sleep
c. Watching television
d. Drinking caffeine

53. Which of the following skills is an example of striking with a long-handled implement?

a. Pickleball ground strokes
b. Tennis forehand
c. Hockey pass
d. Racquetball backhand

54. Which of the following is NOT a commonly cited issue with fitness testing in physical education?

a. It does not increase learning.
b. Standardized fitness tests lack validity.
c. It does not lead to lifetime physical activity engagement.
d. It is often a negative experience for students.

55. Heart disease is the number one killer in the United States. Which activities have the greatest impact on reducing heart disease risks?

a. Jogging, swimming, cycling
b. Bodyweight training
c. Circuit training
d. Anaerobic training

56. While welcoming students into his homeroom class for the day, Mr. Gonzalez notices a student who is typically happy and easygoing seems unusually withdrawn. Later that day, he sees several bruises on the student during recess. Which of the following meets the requirements of Mr. Gonzalez reporting suspected child abuse as a mandated reporter?

a. Mr. Gonzalez directly reports the concern with the state authority.
b. Mr. Gonzalez shares his concern with his team teacher so they can monitor the student.
c. Mr. Gonzalez calls the parents after the school day to ask if his suspicions are true.
d. Mr. Gonzalez asks the student if they are being abused at home.

57. Among the components of health-related physical fitness, ______ is the bridge between _____ and _____.

a. Muscular endurance; muscular strength; cardiovascular endurance
b. Cardiovascular endurance; muscular strength; muscular endurance
c. Muscular strength; cardiovascular endurance; muscular endurance
d. Cardiovascular endurance; body composition; flexibility or mobility

58. A student athlete bench presses in order to target his chest and arm muscles and does squats to target his leg and lower back muscles. This is an example of which exercise science principle?

a. Overload
b. Specificity
c. Adaptation
d. Progression

59. Regarding indications that a student should be evaluated to determine eligibility for adapted physical education (APE), which of the following (in addition to referral) correctly states a criterion?

a. The student performs at his or her ability level in group settings but not on an individual basis.
b. The student's social behaviors impede his or her or others' learning more than half of class time.
c. The student has scored below average in one part of the state physical fitness test.
d. The student scored one standard deviation low on the norm-referenced test used.

60. James' heels lift during the down phase of his squat. Which of the following identifies the issue and an exercise to help James keep his heels on the floor?

a. lack of dorsiflexion; toe raises and drops
b. lack of hip flexibility; deadlifts
c. lack of plantar extension; heel raises
d. lack of knee strength; lunges

61. During early childhood, children especially need ______ in their diets to support rapid bone growth.

a. Magnesium
b. Calcium
c. Potassium
d. Starches

62. Body mass index (BMI) calculates an individual's proportion of body fat to height and weight. Which of the following BMI ranges corresponds to a normal body composition?

a. 18.5 or less
b. 25.0 to 29.9
c. 18.5 to 24.9
d. 30 or more

63. The teacher would like to teach the movement concepts effort, relationships, and spatial awareness. Which of the following activities are recommended to develop these concepts?

a. Stationary movements
b. Balancing on the balance beam
c. Fitness activities
d. Animal walks

64. Of the following statements, which is true about aerobics?

a. Aerobics originally focused on the flexibility of the body.
b. Aerobics originally focused on the strength of the muscles.
c. Aerobics originally focused on cardiorespiratory endurance.
d. Aerobics originally focused on one thing as it still does today.

65. Which of the following methods would be LEAST useful for assessing student performance of physical education skills?

a. Observational checklists
b. Rating scales of skill level
c. Written-response exams
d. Performance data graphs

66. A coach realizes that a player who fatigued early during the soccer game did not perform the pre-season workouts. Which of the following is an effective discipline strategy?

a. Having the player run laps
b. Having the player perform push-ups
c. Having the player set goals
d. Having the player sit out the next game

67. Which of the following activities utilizes maps and compasses for accurate navigation?

a. rock climbing
b. orienteering
c. cross country
d. abseiling

68. Which of the following is an example of integrated physical education?

a. Allowing students to choose curricula that relate to classroom content
b. Having students analyze the angles of underhand and overhand throws
c. Inviting specialists to cover topics such as yoga
d. Inviting classroom teachers to teach concepts

69. Which of the following is an effective training program to improve muscular strength?

a. Lift heavy weight, high reps, 1 day a week
b. Lift heavy weight, high reps, 2–3 days a week
c. Lift heavy weight, low reps, 2–3 days a week
d. Lift heavy weight, low reps, 1 day a week

70. Which of the following activities fosters equal opportunities?

a. each student has 10 objects to throw
b. every student has the same target
c. targets consisting of different sizes
d. targets placed at varying distances

71. According to reported experiences, what benefit is there for teachers to use technological applications such as GradeBook Pro?

a. Apps like this enable teachers to quickly calculate grades and create assignment reports.
b. Apps like this reduce final grade disputes by consolidating student data.
c. Apps like this can exponentially speed up the task of taking attendance.
d. Apps like this streamline all of the above tasks and enable teachers to focus their time on teaching.

72. Which of the following statements best describes the impact of verbal feedback compared to nonverbal feedback?

a. Verbal feedback is more effective than nonverbal feedback
b. Verbal feedback is less effective than nonverbal feedback
c. Verbal and nonverbal feedback aid in student learning
d. Nonverbal feedback is the gold standard

73. Which of the following best describes the impact of emotional arousal on motor performance?

a. As arousal increases, performance increases unless arousal becomes too high.
b. As arousal increases, performance decreases.
c. As arousal decreases, performance increases.
d. As arousal decreases, performance decreases unless arousal becomes too low.

74. Which of the following best illustrates generally recommended warm-up and cooldown protocols for secondary students?

a. Ballistic warm-up and static cooldown
b. Static warm-up and dynamic cooldown
c. Dynamic warm-up and static cooldown
d. Dynamic warm-up and ballistic cooldown

75. Which of the following perceptual-motor abilities aids in the development of body awareness?

a. reaction time
b. coordination
c. muscle strength
d. flexibility

76. Which of the following technique cues aids in correcting an overthrown ball during an overhand throw?

a. speed – "Increase the speed of the wind-up motion."
b. release – "Release at 2:00 or 10:00 o'clock."
c. follow-through – "Buckle your seatbelt."
d. foot control – "Take a smaller step towards the target."

77. Ms. Jones collected students' dribbling skills tests data for five years and found many students were not proficient by the end of 8th grade. Which of the following is a logical next step for Ms. Jones to take to improve student dribbling outcomes?

a. Accepting that not all students will meet outcomes
b. Introducing dribbling skills sooner
c. Evaluating her instructional skill cues
d. Providing after-school instruction

78. Which kinds of objects are most suitable for an activity meant to support development of spatial awareness?

a. A balance beam or a vault horse
b. Several balls with different sizes
c. Different sizes of boxes or hoops
d. A gymnasium or big empty room

79. Which of the following results suggests a high level of health-related fitness for a 16-year-old female?

a. BMI = 30; VO^{2}max = 40; push-ups = 20
b. BMI = 25; VO^{2}max = 35; push-ups = 15
c. BMI = 20; VO^{2}max = 40; push-ups = 20
d. BMI = 15; VO^{2}max = 35; push-ups = 15

80. A century of research into motor development has yielded four major principles. Which choice most accurately reflects one of these principles?

a. Children are like adults, only smaller.
b. Children differ completely by gender.
c. Good things are earned.
d. Children have perfect bodies, or not.

81. Recognizing and understanding the significance of regular physical activity to healthy lifestyles is an objective most appropriate to which grade levels in public schools?

a. Grades EC-K
b. Grades K-2
c. Grades 3-5
d. Grades 6-12

82. The teacher blows the whistle one time for students to start activities and uses "freeze" to stop activities. Which of the following strategies is the teacher engaging in?

a. instructional cues
b. transition cues
c. focus cues
d. equipment management cues

83. Which of the following best explains the purpose of using instructional models in physical education?

a. To structure activities for learning
b. To complement the standards
c. To meet all students' needs
d. To simplify planning

84. When using an assessment instrument meant to measure aerobic endurance, physical education teachers find that maximum student repetitions are limited not by their becoming winded but by specific muscle fatigue. After obtaining the same results over repeated administrations, they conclude that this test measures muscular endurance instead. What have they discovered about this test?

a. The test is neither a reliable nor a valid test.
b. The test is a valid test, but it is not reliable.
c. The test is a reliable test, but it is not valid.
d. The test is valid and reliable, but it has been misused.

85. Choosing the appropriate skills is critical in team sports. Which teaching model is best suited for developing decision-making skills during gameplay?

a. Sport education model
b. Tactical games approach
c. Cooperative learning
d. Direct instruction

86. Which statement is correct in regard to how including students in instructional decisions affects student motivation for learning?

a. Students perceiving teacher control of instruction tend to develop internal motivations.
b. Students perceiving ownership of content and learning have more external motivation.
c. Students perceiving some control of learning are more likely to be internally motivated.
d. Students perceiving that teachers control all instruction are unaffected by punishments.

87. Throughout the school year, the teacher randomly teaches dances submitted by students at the beginning of the school year rather than focus solely on the recommended dances, e.g., square dance, in the curriculum. Which of the following concepts is the teacher promoting?

a. self-efficacy
b. diversity
c. choice
d. autonomy

88. Regarding communication with athletes, which statement is recommended by experts for coaches to consider?

a. Coaches must not only get athletes' attention but also explain, so athletes understand easily.
b. Coaches must determine if athletes understood them but not whether they believed them.
c. Coaches must get athletes to understand and believe, not necessarily accept, what they say.
d. Coaches must disregard athletes' individual and group nonverbal cues for controlling them.

89. Concerning the impacts of various resources on student physical education (PE) outcomes, what has research shown?

a. Class size and student–teacher ratio correlate inversely with activity levels, time, safety, and learning.
b. Students receive a higher quantity and quality of PE from teachers who also teach different subjects.
c. Student physical activity is the same whether PE curriculum is based on educational standards or not.
d. PE facilities and equipment are valuable resources but do not change the amount of student activity.

90. Which of the following are impacts that gang involvement can have on adolescent student learning, development, and growth?

a. They protect members from other gangs and adult violence.
b. They meet needs for identity, belonging, rules, and direction.
c. They can end school, jobs, freedom, and life via criminal acts.
d. They have all these impacts on student learning, development, and growth.

91. The principal notices that students with disabilities are sitting on the sidelines during physical education because the teacher indicated it was too difficult to change her plans to meet all students' needs. Which of the following laws of inclusion did the teacher violate?

a. Individuals with Disabilities Education Act
b. Individualized Education Program
c. Adapted Physical Education
d. Family Educational Rights and Privacy Act

92. According to national physical education (PE) standards, to show respect, which of the following should PE teachers do to address a student's behavior problem?

a. The teacher describes the student's behavior, why it was disruptive, and solutions for the problem.
b. The teacher has a classmate describe the behavior, why it was disruptive, and solutions for the problem.
c. The teacher has the student describe the behavior, why it was disruptive, and solutions for the problem.
d. The teacher avoids discussing it but provides concrete consequences and solutions for the problem.

93. Jennifer, a student with visual impairment, has difficulty seeing the colors on the archery targets. Which type of adaption should the teacher consider?

a. a task-specific adaptation
b. an equipment-specific adaption
c. a boundary-specific adaptation
d. a task and boundary-specific adaptation

Refer to the following for question 94:

Research shows that exercise lowers the risk of high blood pressure, stroke, and heart disease. In particular, aerobic exercise has been proven to protect the cardiovascular system.

94. What is true about other health benefits of exercise?

a. Exercise lowers the risk of all kinds of cancers.
b. Exercise cannot change the risk of dementia.
c. Exercise lowers the risk for Type 1 diabetes.
d. Exercise lowers the risk of breaking bones.

95. PE teachers must instruct students to monitor their heart rates during and after aerobic exercise. At what time should they instruct students to take their recovery heart rates?

a. After cooling down
b. Right after exercise
c. While cooling down
d. Between exercising

96. A student is having difficulty staying afloat during the swimming unit. Which of the following identifies a potential problem and a solution to the student's issue?

a. The student has increased drag and needs to empty the air in their lungs
b. The student has high buoyancy and needs to empty the air in their lungs
c. The student lacks drag and needs to fill up their lungs with air
d. The student lacks buoyancy and needs to fill up their lungs with air

97. Which of the following best describes the role of balance in agility-based tasks?

a. Balance supports an athlete's stability when moving quickly.
b. Balance supports an athlete's ability to run fast.
c. Balance supports an athlete's ability to use multiple movement skills proficiently.
d. Balance supports an athlete's ability to quickly change directions.

98. How can a PE teacher best use technology like tablet and smartphone apps that record video, including uploading to computers for playback, for the specific purpose of analyzing student performance and progress?

a. Show them video of professional athletes performing skills they are learning.
b. Show them videos of their activity to identify strengths, development needs.
c. Show them video of classmate activity to identify what things they do wrong.
d. Show them video of the class at the end of a lesson as instructional feedback.

Refer to the following for questions 99–100:

Students in physical education participate in an annual dance-off fundraising competition with students in the dance program. The competition involves several performances which require strength and stamina. The students are practicing the dance routines for 60 minutes, five days a week. However, the teacher notices at the end of the first week that several students are jerky in their movements during the performance.

99. In addition to practicing the dance routines, which of the following conditioning protocols should the students utilize?

a. Aerobic training two days a week
b. Strength training two days a week
c. Aerobic training five days a week
d. Strength training five days a week

100. On which movement concept does the teacher need to focus to help students move more smoothly?

a. Force
b. Time
c. Flow
d. Levels

101. Of the four types of diseases—cancers, cardiovascular diseases, diabetes, and respiratory diseases—that cause the majority of deaths from noncommunicable diseases, which risk factor is not common to all four types?

a. Unsafe water
b. Drinking alcohol
c. Poor diet
d. Smoking tobacco

102. For the throwing unit, the teacher decides to teach basketball followed by team handball. Which of the following provides a rationale for this decision?

a. Offensive and defensive patterns are the same
b. Both are invasion games
c. Throwing patterns differ
d. Throwing patterns share significant overlap

103. Which of the following methods best improves high complex skill combinations?

a. part practice
b. whole practice
c. whole-part-whole practice
d. small-sided games practice

104. During sporting events, spectators are expected to adhere to rules. Although they are not players, why is their compliance with the rules important?

a. To keep the noise level down
b. To ensure that players hear coaches
c. To keep the environment safe
d. To practice sportsmanship

105. Which of the following describes how dances aid in development of respect for diversity?

a. Every student can participate
b. Every student's culture can be included
c. Every locomotor movement can be used
d. Every non-locomotor movement can be used

106. Which of the following descriptions is most applicable to learning standards for PE students in grades 9-12?

a. Students show the ability to explore fundamental locomotor and non-locomotor skills.
b. Students are capable of demonstrating the mature forms in locomotor and non-locomotor skills.
c. Students can apply the mature forms of motor skills in specialized sports, dance, and gymnastics.
d. Students use locomotor, non-locomotor, manipulative skills in sports, dance, and gymnastics activities.

107. In a public school's PE risk management and emergency procedure plans, which is typically among the provisions?

a. If any students are injured, the school nurse offers the initial first aid.
b. All physical educators carry emergency first aid kits during PE classes.
c. Not all physical educators need have current first aid and CPR certificates.
d. PE teachers may not know which students lack treatment permission.

108. Of the following, which most accurately represents an aspect of the relationship between nutrition and fitness?

a. Exercising regularly and energetically enables you to eat anything you want.
b. Eating a diet rich in calcium prevents bone density loss, but exercise cannot.
c. Eating right provides energy for exercise, while exercise can control appetite.
d. Exercising prevents high blood pressure and cholesterol more than diet does.

109. A fifth-grade class is scheduled immediately after a first-grade class. What is the best management system to ensure a safe transition of equipment?

a. End class 10 minutes early for setup and breakdown
b. Alternate between first grade and fifth grade for equipment management
c. Train students to breakdown and set up equipment
d. Use the same equipment for both groups

110. Which of the following body composition measures estimates body fat composition using a person's height and weight?

a. Skinfold calipers
b. Hydrostatic weighing
c. Waist circumference
d. Body mass index

111. In a risk management plan for a school PE program, which division or section would include emergency procedures and accident reports in cases of student injury?

a. Conduct of activities and services
b. Conditions from the environment
c. Management of student behavior
d. Practices of supervision in general

112. Which of the following activities fosters motivation to engage in lifelong physical activity?

a. Grades
b. Fitness testing
c. Self-assessment
d. Ability tracking

113. Which of the following best describes the purpose of rhythmic activities?

a. To learn music tempo
b. To learn how to perform
c. To learn how to control the body
d. To learn the locomotor movements

114. Which of the following is an equitable fitness assessment?

a. standardized fitness testing
b. standards-based fitness goals
c. fitness reflection journals
d. peer-assessments

115. Which of the following is a benefit of elective physical education programs?

a. Ensures enough equipment for all students
b. Caters to the teacher's strengths
c. Students decide their program
d. Helps with non-PE course schedules

116. Ms. Johnson is in a panic because Mr. Oliver took the heart rate monitors she needs for class. Which of the following heart rate monitoring strategies can the teacher use?

a. taking the pulse rate at the radial artery
b. using the talk test
c. checking rate of perceived exertion
d. asking students how they feel

117. Which of the following is a physiological benefit of exercise that helps manage stress responses?

a. it improves mood
b. it enhances positive thoughts
c. it lowers the release of cortisol
d. it increases confidence

118. Which of the following is a non-locomotor movement skill?

a. Skipping
b. Bending
c. Walking
d. Galloping

119. A third grader broke down and had a temper tantrum after having a series of unsuccessful forward rolls. Which of the following factors might be impeding the student's physical development?

a. emotional knowledge
b. emotional self-regulation
c. self-efficacy
d. self-esteem

120. Title IX regulations regarding gender equity in PE stipulate which of the following?

a. Student participation in PE classes may be refused or required by gender.
b. Student participation in PE classes may not be subject to ability grouping.
c. Student participation in body contact sports may not be separated by sex.
d. Student participation in PE skills must be assessed by unbiased standards.

121. Ms. Jones informed LaTonya that she did a good job keeping her eye on the ball but needed to strike the ball in front of her body. She pointed to the area that LaTonya should strike the ball and followed by stating, "strike sooner and keep up the great job tracking the ball." Which of the following feedback methods did Ms. Jones illustrate?

a. the corrective method of feedback
b. the constructive method of feedback
c. the sandwich method of feedback
d. the single channel method of feedback

122. During the dance unit, students alternate between leading and following to develop which of the following social skills?

a. leadership
b. teamwork
c. loyalty
d. inclusion

123. Which of the following is the safest method to evaluate muscular strength?

a. One-repetition max
b. Estimated one-repetition max
c. Repeated performance of an exercise
d. Measuring the range of motion at the joint

124. Which of the following strategies is recommended when selecting weight training activities for beginning students?

a. Utilizing dumbbells
b. Utilizing bodyweight
c. Utilizing a one-repetition max strength test
d. Alternating light and heavy weight

125. If a teacher observes a student frequently coming to school with bruises, which is the best example of the kind of question or statement the teacher should ask the student?

a. "Is somebody hurting you at home?"
b. "Who is it that has been hitting you?"
c. "Tell me how you got those bruises."
d. "Did you fall down and hurt yourself?"

126. Which of the following exercises targets the abdominal muscles?

a. Air bicycle
b. Alien squat
c. Axle deadlift
d. Dumbbell curl

127. Mr. Jackson planned activities in great detail to ensure student learning and engagement, but it wasn't easy getting his students from one activity to the next. What should Mr. Jackson consider the next time he teaches this lesson?

a. Form student groups ahead of time.
b. Account for transition time.
c. Wait until he has the students' attention.
d. Refrain from using that lesson plan.

128. What is the meaning of the "10:1 Rule" relative to early childhood behavior management?

a. For every 10 negative comments/corrections, give 1 positive comment.
b. For every 10 well-behaved students, there is 1 poorly behaved student.
c. For every 1 new behavior to be learned, 10 repetitions are necessary.
d. For every 1 negative comment/correction, give 10 positive comments.

129. Which of the following is classified as a non-locomotor skill?

a. Running
b. Jumping
c. Climbing
d. Dodging

130. Which of the following is not a physical effect of the furry outside of tennis balls?

a. The fur causes a tennis ball to accelerate slower when struck.
b. The fur allows the player to impart spin to the ball when swinging.
c. The fur causes air drag on the ball, slowing its speed during play.
d. The fur allows for extra grip on the ball.

Answer Key and Explanations for Test #2

1. B: Exit routes should be included and posted as part of the teacher's emergency plan. The emergency plan may include the first aid kit's location and how to treat injuries, but the first aid kit alone (A) is not a part of an emergency plan. Student medications (C) such as an inhaler or epi-pen, should either be with the student, school nurse, teacher, or central location for easy retrieval. The teacher should be aware of students with medical conditions, ensure that students have appropriate medications before activity engagement, and be certified in first aid and CPR. Medical conditions and how to treat them are generally in the teacher's notes or lesson plan (D), but generally not included in the emergency plan—as emergency plans are designed to address general, school-wide emergencies, such as a fire or an intruder, and the steps to take, rather than addressing specific needs of individual students.

2. C: Video analysis allows for continued review of kinesthetic skills where the performer can see what they did well and what needs improvement. Video analysis along with verbal feedback has shown the most effective in improving kinesthetic skills. The sandwich method is a feedback delivery method that sandwiches corrective or critical feedback with positive feedback. The type of corrective feedback given will determine if it is useful. The knowledge of results is terminal feedback that provides input on the outcome, whereas knowledge performance feedback positively impacts motor skills. Knowledge of feedback is awareness of the feedback provided—no matter the type.

3. A: Typically developing students should be able to hit a ball pitched by another by the end of the third grade. They should be able to demonstrate sport-specific movement skill combinations, e.g., catch, dribble, and pass a basketball to a moving partner (B) by the end of the fourth grade. They should be able to jump a rope twirled by others (C) by the end of kindergarten. They should be able to jump a rope they twirl themselves (D) by the end of the second grade.

4. A: Students in grades 9-12 can be expected to utilize dynamic balance to make transitions in gymnastics routines and between movements in specific sports. Students in grades 6-8 can be expected to create a sequence of balances using counterbalances and counter-tensions, and to demonstrate this sequence (B). Students in grades 3-5 can be expected to demonstrate a variety of static and dynamic balances, by themselves or with others (C). Students in grades K-2 can be expected to demonstrate static balance using different body parts, shapes, and support bases (D).

5. A: Descriptive feedback, like choice A, provides feedback that describes what the student is currently doing. It can reinforce what the student is currently doing, but it does not attempt to correct an error. Each of the other answer choices are examples of prescriptive feedback, which helps students learn motor skills correctly by telling the student what to do or how to do it.

6. B: PE teachers should design, choose, modify, and sequence game activities not simply to keep students busy (a) or prevent misbehavior (c). While they should ensure these activities promote maximum student enjoyment, this should not be the only purpose without any learning goals (d). Rather, they should aim for activities to promote student fitness, skill improvement, practice in sport-specific skills, AND enjoyment (b).

7. B: The change in heart rate is likely a decrease in fitness. An increase in heart rate may indicate a respiratory condition or infection, but the normal resting heart rate range is 60 to 100 bpm. Hence, a resting heart rate of 83 bpm is within normal limits. A consistent resting heart rate above 100 bpm is likely tachycardia, or fast heart rate. It could indicate illness or a life-threatening condition.

In this case, the teacher should inform the student, notify a parent or guardian, and school nurse if available. A fast heart rate is not likely an indicator of heart disease. High blood pressure and obesity are risk indicators of heart disease.

8. D: The Federal Education Records and Privacy Act (FERPA) is the law that protects students' medical and personal information from dissemination without parental and/or children's consent. Individuals with Disabilities Education Act (IDEA) is a law that ensures that students with disabilities receive a quality education that includes providing appropriate accommodations for student success. Attention Deficit Hyperactivity Disorder (ADHD) is a mental health condition where individuals have difficulty focusing that is accompanied by hyperactive behaviors that can impede learning. The Health Insurance Portability and Accountability Act (HIPAA) is a law that protects patient privacy of medical information.

9. D: Variation and goal setting have been shown to decrease boredom, promote engagement, and foster enjoyment in physical activities. Students complain for a variety of reasons—even students who enjoy physical activity. Districts do not generally have a lot of influence in the methods teachers use to teach the curriculum if the standards are being met.

10. D: The Society for Health and Physical Educators (SHAPE) America sets the national K-12 and physical education teacher education standards. The Council for the Accreditation of Educator Preparation (CAEP) is responsible for accreditation of physical education teacher education programs and working closely with SHAPE America. GOPHER is the largest equipment supplier for physical education and has partnered with SHAPE America. The former National Association of Sport and Physical Education (NASPE) is now SHAPE after combining with the American Alliance for Health, Physical Education, Recreation and Dance.

11. B: Metabolic syndrome is a medical condition related to sedentary lifestyles and poor nutritional habits that includes three or more risk factors including obesity, high cholesterol, hypertension (high blood pressure), high glucose (high blood sugar), and excessive fat around the waist. All of these factors occur in a cluster which increases the risk of diabetes, stroke, and heart disease. Hypokinetic diseases are also lifestyle conditions that result from inactivity or sedentary living that include the risk factors of metabolic syndrome as well as osteoarthritis, osteoporosis, some cancers, depression, and lower-back pain.

12. B: The tactical games approach (aka Teaching Games for Understanding, or TGfU) is a model designed to teach students situational awareness, or how to make decisions during game play. This approach allows for students to play the game first, then work backwards to solve problems for common situations or errors. Students develop a collection of options to choose from when confronted with certain situations. For instance, when an offensive player has the ball during an invasion game and is doubled-teamed, the player pulls from the database of effective options rather than freezing up and not knowing how to respond. The teacher tries encouraging students to problem solve rather than tell them the answers as is done during the direct teaching approach. Decisions are made in the Sport Education Model, but they are restricted to the role of the student (coach, scorekeeper, equipment manager) and not specifically to game play. Cooperative learning is embedded in the tactical games approach as students work collaboratively to make team decisions.

13. D: Mirroring is when partners face each other. One partner does what the other is doing, which aids in the development of locomotor and non-locomotor movements as students have an opportunity to "see" and imitate or "mirror" the movement. Mirroring is helpful to unskilled students who can mirror skilled students. Skilled students also benefit from mirroring drills as they can detect and correct errors, which helps both the skilled and unskilled students become proficient. Choice is a strategy used to foster motivation. There are multiple purposes for games, but games allow students to put skills into practice. Equipment aids in the development of movement concepts and manipulative skills.

14. B: Variable practice has been shown to be the most effective in PE and sport settings, as the same game skills are practiced in various situations to mimic real play, e.g., small-sided games. Random practice is mixing up skills in random order, which is similar to variable practice, but the skills differ. Blocked practice focuses on one skill at a time and repeats, which is evident during isolation skills practice. Mental practice is thinking about or rehearsing the skill cognitively, which has been shown to benefit physical skills when used in conjunction with physical practice, but it is not as strong when used independently.

15. A: Hypothermia is a condition when there is a considerable drop in body temperature resulting from exposure to extreme cold conditions or prolonged exposure in cold environments. Exposure to cold water increases hypothermia risk. Hyperthermia is a condition when there is a significant increase from exposure to heat or prolonged physical activity in hot environments. Vasodilation increases blood flow and sweat response to cool the body while training in warm and hot temperatures. Vasoconstriction occurs to decrease blood flow to keep the body warm or reduce heat loss when training in the cold. Cold weather does not cause colds; germs cause colds, which may occur in hot or cold conditions.

16. B: To enhance students' perceived physical competence, it is better for physical education (PE) teachers not to specify how many trials to complete during a certain time period (A) but rather to specify the time period for practicing without requiring any specific number of trials (B). This allows students to focus not on how many times they complete the actions but rather on perfecting their technique. Rather than emphasizing technical errors they make (C), it is better to emphasize which things students do well technically, providing positive reinforcement that increases their motivation to practice. Varying assigned activities is more effective to minimize off-task student behavior than not varying them (D).

17. D: "The student will skip using a mature pattern" is an example of a SHAPE America grade level outcome for students in grade 1, as it is explicit about what students are expected to do, while "the student will demonstrate motor skills" is a SHAPE America standard that is broad or general. Students will also apply movement concepts and it is hoped that students recognize value in physical activity, but these too are general standards rather than explicit outcomes.

18. D: The chronic bacterial outbreaks are likely attributed to failing to take a shower after physical education class. Cleaning the body after moderate to vigorous physical activity reduces bacteria growth thus lowering the risk of disease. Coughing is usually associated with a cold, which is a viral infection. Most conditions that result from skin-to-skin contact or rolling around on mats are viral or fungal. Ringworm is a common example.

19. A: The Society for Health and Physical Educators (SHAPE) America sets the national K-12 and physical education teacher education standards and each state-level SHAPE equivalent adopts these standards. Council for the Accreditation of Educator Preparation (CAEP) is responsible for accreditation of physical education teacher education programs and working closely with SHAPE America that also sets the health and physical education standards for teacher education programs. HPE is the acronym for health and physical education used in some programs. The Every Student Succeeds Act (ESSA) is a law designed to ensure equal opportunities for all students, including health and physical education.

20. A: The objective is like a public declaration for all to see – not only the students, but also other teachers, administrative staff, and parents who want to know what is going on that day and whether the objective has been clearly communicated to the students. One of the benefits of a clearly written, focused objective is that the teacher knows exactly what to evaluate – did the students learn the objective for the day? Another benefit is that the evaluation works in reverse also – providing a measure for the teacher to judge his/her own effectiveness. It is the primary purpose of an objective to focus the students on what they are to learn that day; in addition, a well-written objective might also motivate students to want to learn the day's lesson.

21. C: Getting closer to the net is an appropriate modification as it only requires the student to adjust rather than lowering the nets, which is a difficult, time-consuming task. The student can start closer to the net and take steps back after success to get comfortable with the motion until they can get the ball over the net from farther distances. During gameplay, balls are returned from every court area, which makes this modification more realistic for gameplay. Lowering the net may alter or develop poor technique when returning to the standard net height. Practicing against a wall can aid in stroke development but is not specific to getting the ball over the net. Watching a peer can improve performance, but it is not a modification.

22. B: Physical education (PE) instructors can address negligence in instruction (A) by ensuring they teach students the correct procedures and protocols for safety and for equipment setup, use, and takedown and ensuring students understand and practice how to execute sport and movement activities beforehand. Because PE classes often are large and getting larger, they can address negligence best in supervision (B) by ensuring they continually and actively supervise students throughout all activities and enlisting students to practice peer supervision in addition to supplement teacher supervision. In transportation (C), teachers and coaches are liable outside of school and must obtain written parental consent; follow all school policies, practices, and procedures; and supervise student behavior on buses. In class environments (D), teachers and coaches must be alert for possible dangerous conditions, which can vary daily, and space students to limit hazards.

23. A: The physical education standards are initially developed by SHAPE America, the largest national physical education organization that sets the standards for K-12 physical education and the Physical Education Teacher Education program (PETE). The state government and state-level physical education organizations adopt and can revise the national standards, which are then disseminated to the state's school districts. School districts and physical education teachers may have their own goals, but their practices must conform to the state requirements.

24. A: To attain the fastest acceleration, a sprinter should keep the center of gravity as high as possible while crouching in the starting block. As the sprinter accelerates, the upper body rises with forward body propulsion. Having the center of gravity lowest (b), between high and low (c), or starting in the full upright body position (d) will allow less speed in accelerating.

25. A: Most communities have parks and recreation centers that provide physical activity programming for children, adults, and families which are usually free, low cost, and/or have sliding scale fees based on income. Parks and recreation leaders have degrees and/or training in providing physical activity services. Some areas have hiking trails but these areas tend to be unsupervised and can be unsafe for children. Special equipment is needed for rock climbing and can be expensive. Some parks and recreation facilities offer indoor rock-climbing walls. Fitness centers are appropriate for high-school-aged students but some are for adults only or require a parental waiver for youth under 18 and require a fee. Many parks and recreation facilities have fitness centers for youth.

26. D: Physical education (PE) teachers must always conduct regular safety inspections of facilities and equipment on a consistent basis. Rather than using extrinsic motivations (A) like external punishments or rewards, PE teachers are advised to enhance intrinsic student motivations to be responsible for learning. When student behaviors are inappropriate, PE teachers should not ignore them (B) but address them immediately. PE teachers do need to obtain and regularly renew certification in cardiopulmonary resuscitation (CPR) and automated external defibrillator (AED) use (C).

27. A: While feedback is important in physical education (PE) instruction, knowing when and when not to provide feedback is equally important to effective teaching. PE teachers need to give feedback to give students specific corrections to incorrectly performed techniques, for example. However, when a task furnishes inherent environmental feedback (B),—for example, a student throws a basketball, and it goes through the hoop—additional feedback may be unnecessary. When a student already has enough experience with a skill (C), sometimes PE teachers need not give them feedback. Also, when a teacher's demonstration enables students to see easily how to perform a skill correctly (D), they may need little or no additional feedback.

28. B: The PE teacher should first check the scene for safety. Next, she would check the spectator for signs of consciousness, e.g., talking, breathing, and pulse. If there is no breathing, the PE teacher would identify and instruct someone to call 911 and include the assessment. If there is an AED available, that request would also be made followed by CPR until the AED arrives, medical personnel arrive, and/or the PE teacher is too tired to continue performing CPR correctly.

29. A: Staying close to the opponent is a common defensive strategy used during invasion games to prevent them from getting the ball/object or to prevent them from shooting the ball/object to score. V-cuts and L-cuts are offensive strategies used to get open. A fake or feign is also an offensive strategy used to slow down the defense. Getting open is an offensive strategy.

30. A: Self-assessment is a self-regulation tool designed to help students evaluate skill development and refine skills. Self-assessment allows students to ascertain the quality of their own performance based on skill cues. They focus on the missed cues to refine the performance. The teacher usually administers a survey or inventory of learning preferences, which helps to plan for instruction. Self-assessment is designed for student growth and should not determine student outcomes because that is the teacher's job. The teacher also administers or determines which summative assessment will be used to establish what was learned.

31. D: When performing the Fosbury Flop, the force applied during the takeoff allows the body to elevate and project over the bar. The arched position of the body, known as the Fosbury Flop, during the jump simulates a projectile motion curve where the center of mass lies outside the body, which makes it easier to elevate and travel over the bar. Torque is a twisting force that causes the body or body parts to rotate around an axis and can generate angular momentum (e.g., a somersault).

32. D: Coach Wheelock is demonstrating low expectations and gender stereotypes of female students despite their role as basketball athletes. He assumes that they would not be able to play with the boys. He also assumes that all boys play rough, which is another gender stereotype. Rules should be in place to ensure safety for all students. As long as the girls can play basketball in class, separating groups by gender would not be considered gender discrimination or favoritism towards the boys.

33. B: A proactive approach to injury reduction would be engaging in a warm-up to increase blood flow to the muscles in preparation of more strenuous work. Identifying exit doors is a proactive safety measure to use as an escape route in the event of a fire, but does not reduce the risks of injuries. Contacting the principal is a reactive measure conducted after an injury has occurred. Students setting up and breaking down equipment is a classroom management strategy.

34. D: An on-site police officer is not a requirement for school-wide emergency response plans. The other options represent minimum requirements.

35. C: The sword in fencing is called a foil. Soccer, cricket, lacrosse, hockey, and baseball use shin guards. Wrestlers wear a singlet, and players compete on a large mat. Tumbling and gymnastics also occur on large mats.

36. A: MyFitnessPal, Strava, and Fitbit all allow users to synchronize data with devices or other fitness platforms, such as wearable trackers or partner apps. Syncing enables automatic transfer of information like steps, workouts, calories burned, and nutrition logs, allowing users to monitor their health data across multiple tools. B is incorrect because extensive recipe databases are mainly associated with MyFitnessPal. C and D are incorrect because audio coaching and guided workout video libraries are not standard features across all three apps.

37. A: An equitable instructional practice is to allow the student to move closer to the net to meet diverse learners' needs. Lowering the net would be inequitable to the other three students capable of serving in the normal position. Allowing the partner to serve prevents the shorter student from developing and participating, which is an inequitable practice. Badminton is a fast sport that requires quick movements and reaction time, so a box would be unsafe as it would be on the court preventing movement and increasing the risk of injury.

38. C: Watching other classmates perform a skill helps students build confidence. Skill cues help with the understanding of how to perform a skill but do not build confidence independently. Many students are not competitive, and competition has shown to hinder confidence for novice learners. Positive self-talk may help build confidence, but negative or overly critical self-talk hinders confidence and skill performance.

39. D: Circuit training is an effective method to teach all of the health-related activities when there is limited time, as dedication to each component can be included. Resistance training can be included in circuit training, but performed independently, it addresses only muscular strength and muscular endurance—two health-related fitness components. Interval training is inherent in circuit training as there is a particular time or amount of activity followed by transitional rest periods. Intervals can also be explicit within circuit training but do not guarantee coverage of all health-related fitness components independently and are often used for cardiovascular fitness. Fartlek training is speed training for running and does not provide well-rounded coverage of the health-related fitness components.

40. D: Trunk lifts will help Daniel strengthen his core, including the lower back. Lat pulls train the latissimus dorsi, which is the large part of the upper back. One-arm rows also train the latissimus dorsi and the rhomboids or the upper inner parts of the back. The seated row also targets the latissimus dorsi and rhomboids.

41. A: Although some skills are harder to break down, in general, PE teachers should demonstrate a skill as whole-part-whole, i.e., demonstrate the whole skill first; then break it down and demonstrate its components; and then demonstrate it as a whole again, rather than only demonstrating the parts (b) or only the whole (c). They should also give fewer, not more, cues (d), e.g., 1-3 at a time, according to student developmental levels and skill complexity.

42. A: Some students and others may be pleasantly surprised to learn that overweight and obese individuals can lower their risk of related diseases by losing only 5-10 percent of their existing body weight. In addition, overweight (not obese) individuals whose waist measurements are not disproportionately large and who have one or no other risk factors may need only maintain rather than reduce their weight.

43. C: Posture has played an equally significant role in classical and contemporary theories of motor development. In classical theories attributing motor skill development to neuromuscular maturation, increasingly vertical posture was evidence of babies' progress as their cerebral cortices developed more control over their abilities to overcome gravitational pull. In contemporary theories attributing motor development to dynamic systems and relationships between perceptions and actions, posture became the stable biomechanical basis for action and was evidence of learning about new perception–action systems. Hence, posture was not more important to either classical theories (A) or contemporary theories (B). Neither did these theories regard its role in motor development as minor (D).

44. C: According to the Centers for Disease Control and Prevention (CDC), childhood obesity is defined as having a body mass index (BMI) at or above the 95th percentile. Obesity rates in young children have increased in recent years and are strongly correlated with several short- and long-term negative health consequences. Children that suffer from obesity often experience developmental difficulties across various domains, including limited ability to engage in physical activity, impaired cognition, and social and emotional harm. Further, individuals that are obese in childhood are more likely to remain so as adults and are at risk for serious health complications, such as diabetes, bone and joint issues, high blood pressure, and cardiovascular disease. Lifestyle factors such as poor nutrition, excess calories, and lack of exercise have been identified as some of the greatest contributors to childhood obesity. Early education and emphasis on the importance of health and wellness can be highly effective in helping to prevent childhood obesity. This includes teaching young children how to make responsible food choices, incorporating movement into daily learning experiences, modeling positive attitudes toward health and physical activity, and communicating with families about ways to reinforce these concepts at home. In doing so, teachers can encourage and instill practices within students that can become lifelong habits for maintaining health, fitness, and overall wellness.

45. C: Planks work the trunk (abs and back), and squats work the quadriceps. Curl-ups train the abdominals, and deadlifts train the hamstrings. Knee lifts train the abdominals and quadriceps, and seated rows train the back muscles (lats and rhomboids). Twists work the abdominals, and leg curls work the hamstrings. There are synergistic muscle groups involved in most exercises, but the dominant muscle groups worked are identified.

46. B: Distress is a form of stress that leads to anxiety or extreme nervousness. Eustress is positive stress and is often felt prior to a physical performance (game, dance, or music recital); however, these events can also bring on distress—usually among individuals with low competence or confidence. Physical stress can be positive (physical activity needed for positive physiological adaptations) and negative (headache, pain). Fight or flight is a stress response. Some avoid dealing with stressful situations (flight), while others persevere (fight). Allowing students several opportunities to practice fitness tests helps reduce stress and anxiety.

47. A: Teambuilding activities, including trust falls, are often incorporated before sports practice or at the beginning of a physical education course to foster teamwork. One has to depend on another to meet a goal (e.g., to not fall). Taking turns and rotating team captains can create a balance in opportunities to engage, but teamwork will not develop automatically without a common goal or objective. It is controversial when students pick their teams because low-skilled, overweight, and obese students who frequently get picked last and face embarrassment tend to develop negative feelings towards physical activity. It is recommended that teachers pick teams to balance ability and safety.

48. A: The teacher should recommend that this student engages in interval training with heart rate tracking to challenge the student to increase intensity in short bouts, which has improved cardiovascular fitness similar to endurance activities. Teachers can use the heart rate to determine criteria for high and low intensities. A pedometer is good for tracking steps but not intensity, and this student has an intensity issue. Students should be taught about the benefits of cardiovascular health, but awareness alone is not sufficient and does not provide a goal for the student. Engaging in activity for longer periods of time may increase the intensity, but there is limited time in physical education classes, and higher intensities in short bouts are more realistic. Research has also shown that students in physical education courses prefer high-intensity interval activities over long endurance activities.

49. C: Free weight exercises help improve flexibility and posture. These exercises are conducted using a full range of motion at the joints and strengthening muscles that aid in keeping the body in an upright position. Isometric exercises are those that use static positions that require muscular resistance, such as wall sits and planks, and do not allow for a repeated range of motion. Running reduces flexibility as the repetitive motion strengthens but tightens the muscles.

50. B: When participation in PE or other physical activities is impeded by student insecurities (A), this is an example of the impact of psychological factors on motor development and performance. The widespread phenomenon of playing video games to the exclusion of physical ones (B) is the best example of the impact of social factors. Poor home living conditions (C) are an example of the impact of environmental factors. Illnesses and disabilities (D) are examples of health factors.

51. D: Getting rest and eating a meal with carbohydrates will help students prepare for a cross country meet as both contribute to the athlete having more energy and reduced fatigue. Energy from carbohydrates is easier and faster to recruit than energy from fats. The race would be over before fat energy could be used. Rest also allows the body to recover from the muscular stress that occurs during exercise. A practice run one day prior may be disadvantageous as the body will likely experience a faster fatigue rate which can negatively affect performance. A walk-through of the course is recommended to familiarize the runners with the course.

52. B: Getting adequate sleep has been shown to help manage stress as it restores and calms the body and improves concentration, decision-making, and judgment. Most sleep recommendations are 8-10 hours a night. Short naps have also been shown to have similar benefits, including strengthening the immune system and regulating blood pressure that increases during stressful events. Watching television can aid in escaping stress, but it can have an adverse effect and increase stress depending on what is viewed and the length of screen time. Drinking caffeine has been shown to increase the stress response and interfere with sleep quality. Drinking one glass of red wine has shown stress reduction benefits, but over indulgence of alcohol interferes with sleep quality and duration. Over indulgence of alcohol can also lead to alcohol dependence and alcoholism.

53. C: Long-handled implements are designed for adult bodies. Long-handled implements also have levers (tool or a part of the body that helps push, pull, or lift an object) that are longer and further away from the body such as the end of a hockey stick or golf club, which makes these skills more difficult for children. Skills that use long-handled implements are generally taught after striking with short-handled implements (tennis, pickleball, racquetball) as these levers are shorter and closer to the body, thus making it easier to manipulate and apply force to the object.

54. B: Fitness testing is a contentious and commonly debated issue in physical education because it has been shown to be a negative experience for many students, especially if they are unfit, overweight, or obese. Fitness testing has not increased learning or lifetime physical activity engagement, and implementation is often not tied to educational outcomes. Despite these criticisms, standardized fitness tests are generally considered valid.

55. A: Aerobic activities including jogging, swimming, and cycling have been shown to have the greatest impact on reducing heart disease risks. Engaging regularly in these activities increases blood flow through the arteries, reduces blood pressure, and helps with maintaining a healthy body weight. Bodyweight training is a type of resistance training using the body. While bodyweight exercises can include aerobic activities (e.g., jumping jacks), results are not as impactful as jogging, swimming, and cycling unless done using a high-intensity interval training (HIIT) format. Circuit training has similar outcomes as bodyweight training and has benefits to heart health by moving from exercise to exercise, but aerobic activities are specific to training the cardiovascular system.

56. A: Mr. Gonzalez may satisfy the reporting requirements by sharing his concerns with the state authority. This rule varies slightly from state to state, as some states require teachers and other mandated reporters to report directly to the investigative authorities (DFPS, CPS, or another state agency), while other states may allow for schools to have a single representative who files all reports to the state authorities. While some states allow for delegation of reporting to the school's representative, it is *always safe* to directly report the suspicion of abuse, neglect, or exploitation directly to the state. The state is generally responsible for investigating the matter once reported. The state may then contact the police, talk to the student, or speak with faculty and staff. Mr. Gonzalez should not go to his team teacher since they would have the same obligation to report their concerns to the counselor or an administrator at the school. He should not contact the parents after school because this could cause further harm to the student if the child is being abused. Mr. Gonzalez should not ask the child if they were abused because that is better handled by people who have been trained in how to ask sensitive questions, and it is best to not make the child relive potentially traumatizing events more than is absolutely necessary.

57. A: Muscular endurance is the bridge between muscular strength and cardiovascular endurance. In order to exercise long enough to condition the cardiovascular system to a fit level, one must first have or develop enough muscular endurance. Muscular strength alone determines how much force the muscles can exert at one time, but muscular endurance determines how long the muscles can work.

58. B: In exercise science, the principle of specificity means that, to improve certain body parts, muscles, or sports movements and techniques, one must exercise those specific parts, muscles, or movements and techniques. Exercising the lower body will not strengthen the upper body or vice versa. Specificity also means that one must practice football skills, for example, to improve in football rather than only exercising for general body conditioning: The latter may be required for and benefit playing football but will not improve specific football skills—only practicing those skills specifically will. The principle of overload (A) means extra or unaccustomed stimuli is required to make the body respond beyond its normal levels. While overloading is required to make progress in strength and hypertrophy, the principle of overloading is not directly discussed in the question. The principle of adaptation (C) means the body adjusts to processes and demands, making activities easier over time and eventually requiring variation for continuing progress. While strength and muscle growth are adaptations to training, no adaptations are mentioned in the question. No progress (D) is referenced in the question.

59. B: In addition to referrals, criteria indicating that a student should be evaluated to determine eligibility for adapted physical education (APE) include that the student performs below his or her ability level in group settings (A); has social behaviors that interfere with his or her or others' learning more than one-third of class time (B); has scored below average in two or more parts of the state physical fitness test used by the school district (C); and scored 1.5 or more standard deviations below the norm on the norm-referenced test used (D) by the school or district.

60. A: James lacks flexibility in the ankles or the ability to lift his toes towards his shin (dorsiflexion). Toe raises, also known as heel or calf raises, and drops will help James increase his ankle flexibility. The lack of hip flexibility may also cause lifting of the heels, but deadlifts target the hamstrings and lower back. Static and dynamic or a combination of active and passive hip stretching exercises, such as butterflies, kneeling lunges, and pigeons, will help with hip flexibility. Plantar extension is pointing the toes downward, which is not an issue for James as his toes must contact the floor for the heels to lift. Poor knee strength is the weakness in the muscles surrounding the knee, which would prevent James from performing the squat correctly. Side, lateral, and reverse lunges, step-ups, and wall-sits at 90 degrees help strengthen the knee's muscles.

61. B: Early childhood is a period of rapid bone growth, so young children need calcium in their diets. Nutritionists recommend serving young children 2-3 daily servings of dairy products and/or other foods high in calcium. Young children need adequate levels of magnesium and potassium, but these do not support rapid bone growth as directly as calcium. They do not generally need extra starches.

62. C: A BMI of 18.5 to 24.9 is classified as a normal, healthy proportion of body fat to height and weight. A BMI of 18.5 or lower (a) is considered underweight, i.e., insufficient body fat. A BMI of 25.0 to 29.9 (c) is classified as overweight, i.e., excessive body fat. A BMI of 30 or higher (d) is classified as obese, i.e., extremely excessive body fat.

63. D: Animal walks are recommended to teach these movement concepts as students can draw on prior knowledge of how animals move. Using animals allows students to identify different concepts, such as "moving like a flock of birds," to understand spatial awareness, effort, and relationships. Although stationary movements and balancing can teach some movement concepts, the lack of variety limits what can be taught. Fitness activities can teach some movement concepts, but fitness concepts are more abstract and will likely confuse younger children.

64. C: When Cooper and Potts developed and named aerobics in the late 1960s, it originally focused on the ability of the heart and lungs to use oxygen in sustained physical activity. Cooper was the first to differentiate aerobic capacity from body flexibility (A) and muscular strength (B) and to notice that some people who were very flexible or very strong still did not have good endurance for running, biking, or swimming long distances. Although aerobics initially focused on cardiorespiratory endurance exclusively, today's aerobics classes combine all the elements of fitness (D), incorporating stretching for flexibility and strength training for the muscles along with movements that raise heart and breathing rates for cardiovascular fitness in their exercises.

65. C: Tests on which students must write answers are least useful for assessing their performance of physical education skills, which typically must be physically demonstrated. Observational checklists are more useful as teachers can watch students perform the skills to be assessed and mark whether they can do them or not or mark the degree to which they have mastered them. Rating scales of skill level are more useful as teachers can observe student skill performance and then rate the level of mastery or skill they have attained on a scale with degrees between most and least. Graphs of performance data are more useful as teachers can record numbers of successful demonstrations per session as points and connect these to form a line or curve showing progress over time. Graphs also can include a line indicating a criterion for reference, so performance points can be seen above, below, and at this line.

66. D: An effective strategy is having the player sit out the next game to serve as a consequence for missing the workouts. Running laps or performing push-ups is an inappropriate discipline practice as it associates physical activity with pain and punishment. Setting goals is an effective strategy that can be used to accomplish fitness outcomes but is not a disciplinary measure.

67. B: Orienteering relies on maps and compasses to navigate courses and would be difficult to accomplish without these tools. Rock climbing requires equipment such as ropes, belay devices, and harnesses, as well as some experience to identify appropriate rocks to climb. However, a map or compass is not necessary because rock climbing is upward. During competitive cross-country events, event planners and/or coaches set the courses and they are marked to help runners stay on course. Abseiling or controlled falling, also known as rappelling, is the downward motion that occurs after rock climbing; however, abseiling can occur independently of rock climbing.

68. B: Having students analyze angles of underhand and overhand throws is an example of integrated physical education or cross-curriculum approaches, as the angles of release are a physics concept but taught in a physical education environment. Commonly, schools adopt school-wide initiatives to include cross-curriculum activities to garner a deeper understanding of content. Another teacher teaching non-physical education content is cross-curricular instruction but not integrated within the physical education context. Specialists provide expert training in physical education activities. Student choice does not guarantee integration, and choices tend to be from PE curricula.

69. C: Lifting heavy weight at low reps two to three days a week is an effective training program for a muscular strength goal. High reps are more beneficial for a muscular endurance goal. Strength will also increase with a high rep count, but it will take longer to build strength, as the weight needs to be lighter in order to achieve a high rep count. Muscles need rest for 24–48 hours because the process of muscle repair after a strength training workout aids in strength building. Strength training one day a week may result in minor strength gains, but it is typically not efficient enough to warrant the physiological responses needed for substantially improving muscular strength.

70. A: Having 10 objects to throw is an example of equal opportunity as all students have the same number of opportunities to throw. Having only one target increases wait time and many students will have little to no opportunities to throw at the target. Different sized targets and targets at varying distances are examples of differentiated instruction but do not equalize opportunities to throw at the various targets.

71. D: Teachers report that apps like Apple's GradeBook Pro enable them to use more of their class time actually teaching by reducing the time it takes them to perform administrative tasks. Tasks such as taking attendance (C), calculating grades and assignment reports (A) using standard or weighted grading systems, and displaying and consolidating student data all on one page (B) can all easily be done through apps like these. These apps also enable teachers to add assignments easily, e-mail current attendance and grade status to students, send copies of assignments across classes, quickly take and attach student photos to files, and so much more. Overall, these apps streamline all of these tasks to one place, and they provide greater efficiency of the tasks that used to be cumbersome yet necessary.

72. C: Both verbal and nonverbal feedback aid in student learning and are more effective when used together. The effectiveness of each type of feedback is dependent on the learning style of students. For auditory learners, verbal feedback may be more effective, and for visual learners, nonverbal feedback may be best. Combining verbal, nonverbal, and kinesthetic feedback is ideal, as these accommodate diverse learners.

73. A: As arousal increases, performance increases except when arousal levels become too high or exceed the performer's optimal level of arousal. When arousal levels are too high, performance tends to decrease. Arousal levels vary among individuals, but advanced performers tend to have a higher arousal threshold than novice performers.

74. C: A dynamic warm-up involves low-intensity aerobic activities and mobility exercises to prepare the body for the demands of more intense activities by getting blood flow to the muscles that will be used during the activity. A static cooldown helps return the body back to normal and increase flexibility by holding the stretch for longer periods of time. Static stretching is recommended for elementary-aged students because they are still learning how to move and control their bodies. Ballistic stretching or bouncing should be avoided because they increase the likelihood of overstretching or muscle tears.

75. A: Reaction time is a perceptual-motor ability derived from Fleischman's motor skill taxonomies, including perceptual-motor and physical proficiency abilities. Perceptual motor abilities use the senses (sight, touch, and hearing) to navigate and develop movement. For example, the starting gun in a track event requires the body to hear or see the stimuli to respond/react. Coordination, muscle strength, and flexibility also help develop body awareness, but these are physical proficiency abilities or physiological abilities rather than perceptual-motor abilities.

76. B: The angle of release is the issue when a ball is overthrown. Right-handed throwers should release the ball at the 2:00 o'clock position in front of the thrower. Left-handed throwers should release the ball at the 10:00 o'clock position in front of the thrower. The speed of the wind-up does not impact an overthrown ball. The follow-through will put more speed on the ball and is at a diagonal across the body. Taking a step, in opposition towards the target, generates more power in the throw.

77. C: Ms. Jones should evaluate her instructional skill cues and other teaching practices to determine if they meet the intended outcome or if they need to change to ensure that students are proficient by the end of 8th grade. Dribbling is a skill taught in elementary(B), so students should build on those skills in grades 6, 7, and 8. After-school instruction may be beneficial (D), but it would not be the next logical step as a change in instruction needs to occur prior to this because students could potentially continue to practice poor instructional cues. While not all students will meet the outcomes, the goal is to continue to work towards these outcomes (A).

78. C: Students may go under, over, toward, away from, in front of, behind, and beside (A) and (B), but not inside or outside of these. Students can go into, out of, toward, away from, next to, or in front of (D), but not over, under, and often not behind such rooms. However, with differently sized boxes or hoops (C), they can explore all of these relationships, including going inside and outside of them.

79. C: A healthy BMI is 18.5-24.9 kg/m^2, an excellent VO^{2}max result for teen girls is 39.0-41.9 ml/kg/min, and excellent push-up range is 18-24. BMIs between 25-29.9 are considered overweight, and 30 and above are considered obese. BMIs below 18.5 are considered underweight. BMI interpretations have limitations, where tall individuals or those with large amounts of muscle can be inaccurately classified as overweight when they are not. In these situations, percentage body fat is a better measure of body composition.

80. C: Four major principles of motor development are: children are NOT miniature adults (A); among children, boys and girls are more similar than different (B); children get good things by earning them (C); and nobody, and no body, is perfect (D). (A), (B), and (D) each contradict one of these principles; (C) reflects one of them more accurately than the others.

81. D: Recognizing and understanding the significance of regular physical activity to healthy lifestyles is an objective most appropriate for grades 6-12 in public schools. For grades EC-K (A), recognizing that physical activity has health benefits is more appropriate. For K-2 (B), recognizing the benefits of moderate to vigorous physical activity is appropriate. For grades 3-5 (C), recognizing and applying essential movement concepts and elements for their own sustained participation in physical activities is appropriate.

82. B: The teacher is employing transition cues to start and stop activities and get the students' attention. Transitions are planned and taught. While transition cues aid in instruction, instructional cues are the communications from the teacher to students to help them meet the learning objective. Cues, in general, are designed to get students to focus or pay attention, but the example is specific to transitions. Equipment management cues would consist of the teacher instructing students to gather the equipment, which is direct and explicit.

83. A: Instructional models (TGfU, Sport Ed, cooperative learning) help structure activities for learning. All of the instructional models used in PE are reflected in the national PE standards. No model or standard can meet all students' needs, but teachers can design activities and use strategies to meet the needs of diverse learners. There are formulas and techniques (e.g., bullet points, 5-step planning) that are used to simplify planning, but the models alone are not designed for simplification.

84. C: According to the description, the test is reliable, meaning that it gives the same results every time it is administered, but it is not valid, meaning that it does not measure what it was intended to measure. Therefore, it is not correct that the test is neither reliable nor valid (A). It is not true that the test is valid but not reliable (B) but, rather, vice versa. The test is not both valid and reliable, and it is not simply misused (D); it is actually not valid because it does not test what it means or claims to test but assesses something else instead.

85. B: The tactical games approach (aka Teaching Games for Understanding, or TGfU) is a student-centered model that teaches students to make decisions based on various game-like scenarios. The sport education model is also used during team sports. In the sport education model, students have different roles that include coach, player, equipment manager, scorekeeper, and other roles that are involved in team sports. The student serving as the coach makes the decisions for the players. During direct instruction, the teacher makes all of the decisions. Cooperative learning focuses on student collaboration but can impede motor skill development.

86. C: Students are found more likely to develop internal motivation for learning and achieving in school when they perceive that they have some control over their own learning. Students who perceive that the teacher controls instruction are more likely to develop external than internal motivations (A); students who perceive ownership of their own learning and the content they learn are more likely to develop internal than external motivation (B). When they perceive that teachers control all instruction, students are more motivated by external rewards and punishments (D) than internal factors.

87. B: The teacher is promoting diversity among students as the students' dance preferences are influenced by the students' cultures. Since the students submitted dances at the beginning of the school year, this is not an example of choice. Choice would indicate that the students choose the dance for the day or week, but in this scenario, the teacher is randomly choosing from student submissions. Self-efficacy is the belief that one can perform a skill or task. Autonomy is the freedom and independence to make choices on one's behalf. An example of autonomy in physical education is the freedom to move and choose activities as illustrated in creative movement activities, including dance.

88. C: Experts in coaching communication emphasize that effective communication goes beyond simply delivering information. Athletes need to understand the message and believe it is credible and meaningful. Acceptance or immediate agreement isn't required, as athletes may still question the message, but belief and understanding are essential for learning and trust. Answer A is incorrect because understanding alone isn't sufficient if athletes don't believe in the message. Answer B is incorrect because belief matters in effective communication. Answer D is incorrect because nonverbal cues are critical for understanding and managing athlete responses.

89. A: Researchers have found that smaller class sizes and student–teacher ratios correlate with larger quantities of activity time, activity level, safety, and learning for students, whereas larger class sizes and student–teacher ratios correlate with smaller quantities of student activity times, levels, safety, and learning—that is, an inverse correlation. Studies show that students receive more and better physical education (PE) from teachers who teach only PE rather than dividing their teaching time and attention between PE and other subjects (B). Researchers are coming to increasing consensus that standards-based PE curriculum results in greater student physical activity (C). Well-maintained, safe, appropriate, and aesthetically appealing PE facilities and equipment also are found to increase and improve student activity (D).

90. D: Although most adults know gangs encourage or peer-pressure adolescent members into criminal acts that can end their educations, jobs, freedom, and ultimately lives (C), not everyone realizes gangs also confer certain benefits, e.g., protecting teens against violence from other gangs and adult criminals (A), and meeting needs for behavioral direction, personal identity, group belonging, and rules (B). Adversarial relationships are more secure than complex, equivocal, uncomfortable realities; concrete foes are more beatable than larger, more abstract foes like crime, no opportunities, discrimination, illiteracy, and poverty. Hence, gang involvement both negatively and positively affects adolescent development and learning.

91. A: The teacher is violating the Individuals with Disabilities Education Act (IDEA), which guarantees students with disabilities a quality education. Students with disabilities should be engaged in the lesson and instruction given for learning. Physical education teachers should modify activities so that students with physical or mental disabilities can meet the objectives, which is Adapted Physical Education (APE). The Individualized Education Program is a legally binding plan created by a team of professionals (counselors, school psychologists) with parent and teacher input on strategies that help students succeed, like extended time on assessments, read-aloud tests, and taking notes on a computer. The Family Educational Rights and Privacy Act protects student records. Consent is required if records are disclosed.

92. C: National physical education standards (e.g., SHAPE America's standards for responsible personal and social behavior) emphasize respect, responsibility, and student ownership of behavior. A PE teacher can support these standards by having the student describe their own behavior, explain why it was disruptive, and propose solutions. This promotes reflection, accountability, and respectful problem solving. This standard's example does not advise for the teacher to do these things (A): The student must do them for ownership, responsibility, and understanding of his or her behavior. Neither should the teacher ask a classmate (B) to do them for the same reasons. The standard does not recommend giving concrete consequences and solutions instead of discussing the problem (D).

93. B: An equipment-specific adaptation or modification would be helpful and might consist of using bright colors which should be easier for the student with vision impairment to see. The task remains the same, but the object or equipment is adjusted or modified to meet the student's needs. A task-specific adaptation would change the task itself by moving the student closer to the target; however, the student can shoot the arrow; therefore, the task would not change. The boundaries would remain the same as the student's only issue is seeing the colors on the archery targets.

94. D: Research proves weight-bearing exercise strengthens bones, lowering risk for osteoporosis and associated bone fractures. Exercise lowers risk for colon cancer, breast cancer, and some others, but is not proven to lower risk for every kind of cancer (A). It lowers risk for Alzheimer's-type dementia including memory loss (B), as well as depression. It lowers risk for Type 2 diabetes, not Type 1 (Type 1 has a stronger genetic component, so even physically active children can develop it; however, carefully monitored and controlled exercise helps them manage this condition).

95. A: Recovery heart rate should be taken by feeling the pulse for 15 seconds after cooling down, 5-6 minutes after the last aerobic exercise. It should not be taken before cooling down (b), during cooldown (c), or in between exercises (d). Recovery heart rate should be 120 beats per minute (bpm) or lower for safeness and effectiveness; if higher, the next workouts' intensity should be lowered.

96. D: The student lacks buoyancy and can fill up their lungs with air to help keep them afloat. Emptying the air in the lungs will decrease buoyancy and cause the student to sink. Drag slows down a swimmer and can be caused by wearing clothes or when the body is not in a streamlined position.

97. D: Balance provides stability and control needed for movement tasks. Agility can be defined various ways, but it usually refers to a combination of speed, effort, and ability to change positions and directions quickly. Balance is necessary for all motor skills, but it plays a particularly large role in changing directions in agility-based tasks. One example of use of balance in an agility-based tasks is running cone-drills with fast changes in direction. These types of tasks are impossible to perform well in if the athlete is not in control of their balance.

98. B: A PE teacher can use an app by showing video of professional athletes performing skills the students are learning (a) for demonstrating exemplary technique; showing video of classmates to identify not only errors (c) but also strengths for peer assessment or peer coaching; showing video at the end of a lesson (d) for teaching on the playing field and planning future lessons; and showing students video of their activity to identify their own strengths and needs for development (b) for analyzing their performance and progress.

99. B: To initiate a physiological response to strength training, students should engage in two to three days of strength training specific to dance needs every week using progressive overload. The repetition in the dance performances will maintain or increase stamina and aerobic fitness. Aerobic fitness may be achieved by practicing the dance routine 60 minutes, five days a week.

100. C: The teacher needs to focus on teaching students the concept of flow, which is the contrast between smooth and jerky movements. Force focuses on the amount of effort or intensity of a movement. Time is the rate or speed of a given activity, which can aid in teaching flow by asking students to move at a slow pace, but time is not the concept that needs clarification. The term *levels* addresses the different heights at which a movement is performed.

101. A: Unsafe water is a risk factor for many diseases, but not for all four types of diseases listed. Drinking alcohol, poor nutrition, and smoking tobacco are all risk factors shared in common by all four types of illnesses that cause the majority of deaths from noncommunicable diseases.

102. D: The throwing patterns in basketball and team handball share significant overlap and include the chest pass, overhead pass, bounce pass, and baseball pass. While both sports are invasion games and have similar offensive and defensive patterns, the purpose of this decision was to further work on throwing patterns in a different sporting environment. Some differences include the size of the ball, the number of players (five versus seven), and the frequency and time of dribbling.

103. A: Part practice, or the breaking down of a complex skill like a volleyball spike, has shown to be the most effective method for improving high complex skill combinations. Whole practice or fully completing the skill is best for low complex skills such as running. The whole-part-whole method is ideal for tactical concepts like offense and defense used in team sports where players play the game first. During gameplay, weaknesses are identified, broken down in parts, and practiced before resuming gameplay. Small-sided games allow students to put skills into practice, but mastery of complex skills is unlikely to occur, as the game's pace is too fast; thus, the skill needs to be broken down at a slower rate.

104. C: Spectators need to adhere to the rules to maintain a safe environment for all involved. Rules like no food and drink near gameplay help prevent slipping; keeping a certain distance away from players and the game area help prevent tripping, and following capacity codes allows for easy and safe exit in the event of a fire or another emergency. Keeping the noise level down and practicing sportsmanship are examples of etiquette and not rules that are enforced.

105. B: Cultural and folk dances aid in developing respect for diversity as every student's culture can be included or represented through dance. In addition to the dance steps, students are introduced to the meaning behind dances, and historical and cultural facts that pertain to each culture. There are also dances in pop culture that are associated with certain cultural groups such as contemporary line dances. Locomotor movements are activities that children across diverse groups engage or participate in, but these do not inherently foster respect for cultural diversity. Not all students can dance due to mobile disabilities, but respect for other cultures can be gained by learning about others. Non-locomotor movements are inclusive activities that are utilized in dance but do not foster respect for diversity.

106. D: Exploring the basics of these skills (a) most applies to students in grades K-2. Demonstrating mature forms of these skills (b) most applies to students in grades 3-5. Applying those mature forms in more specialized PE areas (c) most applies to students in grades 6-8. Using these motor skills for activities in these areas (d) most applies to students in grades 9-12.

107. B: School emergency procedures typically provide that injured students are initially offered first aid by physical educators with current first aid certification, and only seen by a school nurse for follow-up as needed (A); that all physical educators carry emergency first aid kits during PE classes (B); that ALL physical educators must have current first aid and CPR certification (C); and that PE teachers and other physical educators have a list of any students who did not return emergency treatment permission forms the first week of school (D).

108. C: Good nutrition provides the body with more energy, which enables and motivates people to exercise. Reciprocally, getting regular exercise can help to control the appetite and prevent overeating. Exercising does not mean you can eat anything you want (A). Both calcium and other nutrients in the diet and weight-bearing exercise can prevent loss of bone density and osteoporosis (B). A combination of exercise and a nutritious diet, not one or the other, prevents high blood pressure, high cholesterol (D), diabetes, and other diseases that unhealthy lifestyles often contribute to or cause.

109. C: Students should be trained to breakdown and set up equipment to speed up transition time. Ending class 10 minutes early is inappropriate because students lose instructional/learning time. Using the same equipment is likely developmentally inappropriate, given the size and strength differences between first and fifth grade, and the content taught should be different. Alternating between groups is likely to cause confusion and disrupt routines, which increases classroom management.

110. D: Body mass index is the most widely used body composition measure that predicts or estimates body fat composition using the formula [weight in kg/ (height in m)^2]. Skinfold calipers measure skinfold thickness to estimate the percentage body fat. Hydrostatic weighing is a direct measure of body fat by comparing weight on land and the amount of water displaced by the body when submerged. Waist circumference is an estimated body fat measure that takes into account only the circumference of the waist.

111. D: In a typical school PE risk management plan, General Supervisory Practices includes subcategories of Risk Management Planning Dimensions; Management of Student Behavior (C) / Rules and Regulations; Security; and <u>Care of Injured and Emergency Procedures</u>. Conduct of Activities and Services (A) includes Adequacy of Instruction and Progress; Use of Warnings and Participation Forms; Maturity and Condition of Participants; and Transportation of Students. Environmental Conditions (B) includes Equipment; Facility Layout; Area and Facility Maintenance; and Health Hazards.

112. C: Self-assessment allows students to take ownership of their learning and fosters intrinsic motivation to learn and engage in physical activities for a lifetime. Grades are extrinsic motivators and have less impact on learning and physical activity engagement. Fitness testing studies show that a large percentage of students dislike fitness testing. Self-assessment of fitness has been shown to be more effective than fitness testing. Ability tracking is what a teacher may do to plan for appropriate instruction, as same-ability grouping has shown the most effective in games and moderate to vigorous physical activity engagement.

113. C: Rhythmic activities like dance and creative movements help students learn to control their bodies. While music is often used, the primary goal is body control. Locomotor, non-locomotor, and manipulative movements are used during rhythmic activities which can aid in the performance of skills, like gymnastics or dance routines.

114. C: Allowing students to reflect on their individual fitness is an equitable approach as students can focus on their personal goals and needs. Students can develop personal goals, create a plan, determine how to assess/track/monitor, and adjust accordingly. Standardized fitness testing and standards-based fitness goals are not equitable as all students are expected to meet a standard not tailored to the individual.

115. C: Elective physical education programs allow students to decide or choose the type of programming. Student choice has been shown to increase student motivation. More focus on students' strengths rather than the teacher's strengths is also a benefit. Equipment is dependent on a budget, but some elective programs might be driven by equipment availability. Equipment, however, should not guide the curriculum or course offerings. Physical education is a part of a holistic educational experience, and the goal is to develop students, not provide scheduling relief.

116. A: Ms. Johnson can have students take their pulse at the radial or carotid arteries to measure heart rate. The talk test helps determine if the activities are too easy or intense, but it does not measure heart rate. The rate of perceived exertion is another tool used to determine or evaluate the intensity of exercises but is not a heart rate measurement. Asking students how they feel is a great tool to check in to assess students' responses to activities but is not a tool to measure heart rate.

117. C: A physiological benefit of exercise is it lowers the release of cortisol–a stress hormone and increases the release of endorphins–happy hormones. These physiological responses promote psychological outcomes or benefits including improved mood, positive thoughts, and increased confidence. Confidence also results from seeing the physical changes the body goes through from engaging in exercise.

118. B: Unlike locomotor movements that consist of traveling from one place to another, non-locomotor movements are stationary movements that include bending, stretching, leaning, balancing, twisting, reaching, pulling, and turning.

119. B: The student has not developed emotional self-regulation, which is the ability to control emotions, usually developed by age six. Emotional knowledge is recognizing the emotional state of another. Self-efficacy is the personal belief or confidence in performing a skill. Self-esteem is how one feels about themselves, which can be high/positive or low/negative.

120. D: Title IX (1972) prohibits sex discrimination in education, including athletics. It stipulates that PE classes may NOT be separate on the basis of gender (a); that students MAY be grouped by ability (b); that students MAY be separated by sex for sports requiring body contact (c), e.g., wrestling, football, boxing, ice hockey, rugby, etc.; and if PE skills are measured using a single standard that affects one sex adversely, another or other standard(s) without gender bias must be substituted (d).

121. C: The sandwich method of feedback puts constructive or corrective feedback between two positive comments or feedback. The sandwich method increases motivation, as constructive or corrective criticism can demotivate students as they tend to view it as negative. The positive comments should be specific and highlight what the student is doing well. The corrective feedback should also be specific and include the desired outcome. Pointing out wrong or incorrect movements can demotivate students. Single-channel feedback is a motor behavior theory which posits that people can only focus on one thing at a time, so it is better not to focus on too many feedback cues at once.

122. A: Students are developing leadership skills by having the opportunity to lead a dance. They are also engaged in taking turns. Although the goal is to perform a dance together, the leader makes all of the decisions and is not reliant on the follower for a successful outcome. Loyalty is the devotion to a person or organization. Inclusion is the practice of including everyone.

123. B: The estimated or predicted one-repetition max (1-RM) is the safest method to evaluate muscular strength because it requires sub-maximal lifts, whereas the 1-RM requires a maximum lift, which increases the risk of injury. Another safe method of evaluating strength is to record the amount of weight lifted over time to see the progress. Repeated performance of an exercise is a better measure of muscular endurance, and measuring the range of motion at the joint is an assessment of flexibility.

124. B: Bodyweight exercises are recommended for beginning students in weight training. Bodyweight exercises reduce the risk of injury and teach students how to move the body for physiological adaptations. After bodyweight exercises, light weights, including dumbbells, are introduced with gradual increases in weight. Students are often directed to select a light weight and perform a few reps and, if too easy, select a heavier weight in small increments until the last two or three reps in an 8-to-15-rep count are challenging. This can be used to conduct a predicted one-repetition max test by using predicted one-rep max calculators. The one-repetition max strength test is not appropriate for physical education as lifting the heaviest amount possible in one-rep increases injury risk. Alternating between light and heavy weight is a training method for muscular strength and endurance goals but is not employed with beginners.

125. C: When a teacher suspects child abuse of a student, he or she should ask the student open-ended questions that both enable and require the student to respond with his or her own content in his or her own words. Teachers should avoid leading questions, which direct the student toward particular content (options A, B, and D) or enable the student to respond with only a "yes" or a "no" (options A and D).

126. A: The air bicycle, done lying on the back, hands behind head, legs elevated, making bicycle-pedaling movements in the air while crunching by alternately touching each elbow to the opposite knee, strengthens the abdominal muscles. The alien squat (b) targets the quadriceps (front thigh) muscles. The axle deadlift (c), using barbells, targets the lower-back muscles. The dumbbell curl (d) strengthens the biceps (inner upper arm) muscles.

127. B: Forming students into groups ahead of time is a good strategy to save time and create balance in groups, but Mr. Jackson's problem was with transitions. Teachers sometimes forget to account for transition time, including starting and stopping procedures and methods used to get from one activity to the next. Transition time should be planned just like activities. Students learn more when they focus on instruction. Mr. Jackson should not give up on the lesson but instead reteach the lesson with transitions factored into the timeframe.

128. D: Relative to early childhood behavior management, the "10:1 Rule" means that for every 1 negative comment or correction one gives to a child, the adults should give that child at least 10 positive comments. Positive reinforcement for desired behaviors is proven to be always more powerful than punishment for undesired behaviors.

129. D: Dodging is defined as sharply changing direction, e.g., away from another player or an object. It is classified as a non-locomotor skill because it does not require running, sidestepping (sliding), jumping, or otherwise moving the body's support base or changing position. Running (A), jumping (B), and climbing (C) are all classified as locomotor skills because they do involve moving the body from point to point in space.

130. A: The primary purpose of fur on tennis balls is to generate backspin when struck. This significantly affects the trajectory and bounce of a tennis ball. Other byproducts of the fur on a tennis ball are increased air-resistance, additional control for the player as they strike the ball, and additional grip on specific surfaces. The fur should have a negligible effect on how fast the ball accelerates when hit.